Reflective Teaching: Becoming an Inquiring Educator

To Elliot,

Thanks for your support over the years.

Jim

Reflective Teaching: Becoming an Inquiring Educator

JAMES G. HENDERSON
Kent State University

Foreword by Nel Noddings

Macmillan Publishing Company
New York

Maxwell Macmillan Canada
Toronto

Maxwell Macmillan International
New York Oxford Singapore Sydney

Cover art: Janie Paul
Editor: Robert B. Miller
Production Editor: Jonathan Lawrence
Art Coordinator: Peter A. Robison
Cover Designer: Thomas Mack
Production Buyer: Patricia A. Tonneman

This book was set in Baskerville by TCSystems, Inc. and was printed and bound by Arcata Graphics/Halliday. The cover was printed by New England Book Components.

Printed in the United States of America

Macmillan Publishing Company
866 Third Avenue
New York, New York 10022

Macmillan Publishing Company is part of the
Maxwell Communication Group of Companies.

Maxwell Macmillan Canada, Inc.
1200 Eglinton Avenue East, Suite 200
Don Mills, Ontario M3C 3N1

Library of Congress Cataloging-in-Publication Data
Reflective teaching : becoming an inquiring educator/James G.
Henderson . . . [et al.].
p. cm.
Includes bibliographical references and index.
ISBN 0-02-353511-3
1. Teaching. 2. Teaching—Case studies. I. Henderson, James
George.
LB1025.3.R437 1992
371.1'02—dc20 91-28900
CIP

Printing: 1 2 3 4 5 6 7 8 9 Year: 2 3 4 5

To my parents for modeling an ethic of caring and a concern for social justice, to my wife Janis for the many lessons in reciprocal caring, and to Norm for the many lessons in wise inquiry. Thanks for the education.

Foreword

Three themes guide this fascinating and practical text: reflection, caring, and inquiry. Henderson and his collaborators have been marvelously consistent in carrying these themes throughout their exposition. They invite teachers to inquire regularly into the learning patterns of their students, their own professional growth, and the reasons for everything that goes on in classrooms. At the same time, they make it legitimate for teachers to care deeply for their students and to spend time building relations of trust. Many young people choose teaching as a profession because they care about children, and this book confirms them in their choice. Teaching does require caring, and caring drives inquiry and reflection—the quest for better, more meaningful connections among teachers, students, and subject matter.

This text presents an unusually rich theoretical background for teachers. But theory is interwoven with a narrative that focuses on caring, commitment, and inquiry. The text is practical and highly readable. It does not try to convince new teachers that research has the answers and all they need to do is apply them. Instead, it stresses the need for teachers to think, try things, and analyze the results. It provides a fascinating account of current educational thought, but that thought is always made problematic. It is presented not as a set of prescriptions, but rather as a set of possible insights and an invitation to explore further.

Readers are introduced to educational theory through the voices of four fictional teachers—each one taking a theoretical line familiar in the traditional literature. Each presents a cogent argument for proceeding from his or her particular perspective, and the charm of this strategy is that each comes across as a caring, sympathetic teacher. No strawpersons are introduced to be blown away by powerful gusts of contrary theories.

Readers are introduced to contemporary educational practice through the voices of two practicing teachers. This dramatic touch should confirm new teachers in their commitment to teaching. Here are real people who describe their continuing enthusiasm for teaching in realistic language. Teaching is not easy. Not every day goes well. Not every student loves or even appreciates the teacher. Not every child is convinced that education is worthwhile. But these educators still love teaching and learning; most of all, they obviously care deeply about children.

I am impressed with the authors' sophisticated yet easy-to-read account of curriculum theory. To get as much as this text offers, one usually has to take a special course devoted just to curriculum theory. But here again, the theory is presented as an integral part of the educational narrative. Indeed, the reader is well prepared for the various curriculum perspectives by the dialogues in preceding chapters.

The book achieves a balance between topics that concentrate on classroom activity and those that address the personal and professional growth of teachers. In the latter category, I especially like the emphasis on service as the heart of professionalism. In an age when so many authors focus on the status characteristics of professions, this reminder that professional life means service is refreshing. It helps us to remember that the professions started as *vocations*—as callings.

The authors encourage new and prospective teachers to learn about cooperative learning by engaging in it. Working together, they can practice collegial professional development and peer coaching. These important exercises give them the opportunity to bring together what they have learned about classroom life and what they aim for in professional life.

Another nice touch is the use of simulated case studies. Modeled on the Harvard Business School case method, teaching cases are presented for discussion. Professors will find the sample case analysis especially useful.

This is a wonderful text: one that captures much of the best of contemporary educational thought, tells a coherent story, and—most important of all—confirms teachers in their hope that teaching really does mean caring. But the text also makes clear that caring in education is not just warm and cuddly feelings about students. It means commitment to continued inquiry and a steady devotion to modes of interaction that will bring out the best self in each student and in each teacher, too.

Nel Noddings

Preface

Did you have teachers who encouraged you to become actively involved in your learning? Did they help you discover relevant meaning in what you were learning? Did they themselves act as students of their own teaching and approach educational problems with an open, questioning mind? Three important principles of good teaching underlie these leading questions:

- The encouragement of active, meaningful learning is central to good teaching.
- Expert problem solving is conducted in an open and inquiring manner.
- The exemplary teacher strives for continuing personal-professional growth.

These principles serve as the guiding framework for this book.

People who have little insight into teaching may assume that achieving professional teaching excellence results from acquiring a technical knowledge base.[1] Think of this knowledge base as a savings account. You deposit your "earnings," or the standardized techniques you have learned, and later withdraw them whenever necessary. Schon (1983, 1987) labeled this assumption "technical rationality." According to this view, a teacher who faces a problem need only select an appropriate technique from a learned repertoire and apply it to solve the problem. Schon points out that, unfortunately, most problems cannot be solved this easily.[2]

> In real-world practice, problems do not present themselves to the [reflective] practitioner as givens. They must be constructed from the materials of problematic situations which are puzzling, troubling, and uncertain. In order to convert a problematic situation to a problem, a practitioner must . . . make sense of an uncertain situation that initially makes no sense. When professionals consider what road to build, for example, they deal usually with a complex and ill-defined situation in which geographic, topological, financial, economic, and political issues are all mixed up together. Once they have somehow decided what road to build and go on to consider how best to build it, they may have a problem they can solve by the application of available techniques; but when the road they have built leads unexpectedly to the destruction of a neighborhood, they may find themselves again in a situation of uncertainty. (1983, p. 40)

Reflective teachers who approach teaching and learning as "uncertain" processes serve as the exemplars for this text. They understand that complex learning problems often require creative solutions rather than standardized techniques. This book aims to help you acquire this insight. It also aims to help you apply this insight in your future career. In a nutshell, this is the text's rationale.

Though the text emphasizes processes of inquiry and reflection, it does not reject the concept of professional knowledge. Only the idea of a standardized technical knowledge base is dismissed. Reflective, inquiring teachers are knowledgeable, but their knowledge base is personalized, self-constructed, and ever-expanding. By utilizing the methods in this text, you too will, over time, build your own personalized and ever-expanding professional teaching knowledge base.

The philosophic tradition of pragmatism[3] supports the idea that learning is a personalized constructivist phenomenon. In his essay *Experience and Education* (1938), John Dewey wrote that "experiences in order to be educative must lead out into an expanding world of subject-matter. . . . This condition is satisfied only as the educator views teaching and learning as a continuous process of reconstruction of experience" (p. 87). This text will help you become an inquiring, reflective teacher by guiding you in this reconstruction process.

Pragmatists such as Richard Rorty (1982) argue that a pragmatic approach to education also involves a sense of historical contingency. They believe that our sense of reality is a social creation dependent on our particular historical period. Because our everyday knowledge of education can change, we should evaluate how previous socially created perspectives on teaching influence our current thinking. Therefore, this book includes several historical interpretations as a vital part of a complex cultural conversation on good teaching.[4]

As you study this text, you will systematically examine an ethically based model of inquiring, reflective practice. This model is not a universal prescription for turning education students into good teachers. Rather, it is a compilation of professional qualities and instructional approaches that most good teachers seem to share. Each individual must determine whether and how to incorporate those qualities and approaches into a personal model of good teaching that satisfies his or her own goals, values, and beliefs.

In other words, the content of this book is designed to be challenged. The text is written in an exploratory and interrogative style to encourage you to build your own professional values. You are invited to become an active student of your own teaching as you examine your past experiences and personal purposes to construct your own professional knowledge. Whether you know it or not, you already carry many ideas, motives, feelings, and images about both good and bad teaching. Exploring your personal, autobiographical baggage will help you determine what type of teacher you aspire to become. This complex learning process requires balancing the personal qualities of humility, honesty, and courage with a far-reaching, self-renewing, and politically aware vision of professional excellence.

Organization of the Text

The book begins with a description of the inquiring, reflective teaching model in chapter 1. In chapter 2 you will discover how two individuals gradually became inquiring, reflective teachers through hard work and courageous commitment to quality education for their students. In chapter 3 you will prepare to practice constructivist learning on yourself. You will also have the opportunity to reflect on the caring, inquiring values associated with good reflective practice. Chapter 3 concludes with autobiographical sketches of four fictitious teacher-characters whose points of view will further your inquiry in succeeding chapters.

In chapters 4 through 6 you will use your past experiences and personal purposes to construct your own professional knowledge on educational problem solving, curriculum leadership, and classroom community leadership. Each chapter opens with a general discussion of the topic. Then the four fictitious teacher-characters, each representing a different historical tradition on teaching excellence, offer their personal views and recommendations. The questions and activities in the Personal-Professional Inquiry section will help you use your own past experiences and personal purposes to construct your own knowledge of each topic. Finally, a Further Readings section recommends additional resources for each chapter.

In chapter 7 you will experience cooperative, democratic educational inquiry through two collaborative activities, collegial professional development and peer coaching. In chapter 8 you will practice reflective teaching on simulated and actual student learning problems. The final chapter delves into the politics of implementing inquiring, reflective teaching.

As you study this book, don't sell yourself short. Whatever your background, you *can* become a reflective teacher and an inquiring educator. You will then serve as an inspirational model for your students. If one day they should consider the questions at the beginning of this preface, they will be able to respond, "Yes, I remember at least one such teacher. . . ."

Acknowledgments

This book is based on a sophisticated conception of teaching that I couldn't have developed without the assistance of three mentors at critical points in my career: Norm Bernier at Kent State University, and Elliot Eisner and Nel Noddings at Stanford University. The book's curriculum design results from three years of action research at two universities. I want to thank the following professional colleagues whose teacher education leadership directly or indirectly provided me with the research opportunity I needed: George Olson, Miriam Schowalter, and Craig Orear at Roosevelt University; and Joanne Whitmore, Jane Applegate, JoAnne Vacca, and Richard Hawthorne at Kent State University. Furthermore, my action research efforts would have been meaningless without receptive students at both Roosevelt and Kent State, and I want to acknowledge their many personal and, at times, inspirational contributions to the design of this book.

I owe a debt of gratitude to my curriculum inquiry colleagues in the Chicago metropolitan area: William Schubert and William Ayers at the University of Illinois in Chicago, George Olson and Mari Koerner at Roosevelt University, and Susan Jungck, Kenneth Kantor, J. Dan Marshall, Shirlee Kessler, Anne Bennison, Pat Hulsebosch, and Carol Melnick at National-Louis University. Our regular seminars together helped me clarify the normative principles underlying this text.

I particularly want to thank John Martins, who is on the faculty at Roosevelt University, for our many conversations on how the curriculum sequence in this text should be conceived. His experience with counseling education, his mature insights into the human condition, and his supportive friendship were critical to the development of this text.

I would also like to acknowledge the many helpful and constructive comments from the peer reviewers: Janet Miller, Hofstra University;

Edmund Short, Pennsylvania State University; John Litcher, Wake Forest University; J. Gary Knowles, University of Michigan; David Armstrong, Texas A&M University; Robert Bullough, University of Utah; Paul Cook, Brigham Young University; Alan Tom, University of Arizona; and William Johnson, University of Illinois at Urbana–Champaign.

I want to acknowledge the many personal contributions to this text. Though the book's overall conception is mine and should not be blamed on anyone else, it is the culmination of many collaborative efforts. Carol Melnick of National-Louis University authored chapter 2, Thomas Barone of Arizona State University authored chapter 5, Mari Koerner of Roosevelt University authored chapter 6, and Patricia Hertel of Truman College authored the cases in chapter 8. All four of my collaborators demonstrated the genuine spirit of professional cooperation, and this book is a testament to the possibilities of teacher educators working together to develop and implement reflective teaching programs. Furthermore, the following undergraduates volunteered considerable time and effort to compose the inquiry examples that are dispersed throughout the text: Nancy Pines, Paul Wilm, and Laurie Schmidgall of Roosevelt University, and E. Andrew Derer, Jr., Alicia Tarr, and Jean Hackenbracht of Kent State University.

I want to offer a special word of gratitude to Dale Anne Hambrecht for her careful and thoughtful editing. A compositional challenge of this book has been the application of curriculum theory to specific preservice professional activities. This application requires the use of simple and clear language that conveys the subtle and sophisticated spirit of professional caring, reflection, and inquiry. Dale's editing recommendations were consistently sensitive to this challenge.

Finally, I wish to acknowledge Robert Miller, Senior Editor at Macmillan, for his support and vision over the past two years. Despite a market dominated by technical books on teaching, he understood the importance of producing a teacher education text that focuses on personal-practical knowledge, teaching ethics, professional pluralism, and democratic values. I could not finish on this note without duly acknowledging the mistress of history (and Jonathan Mirsky and Crane Brinton, who introduced me to her). Being born a late-20th-century American means learning to live comfortably within the confluence of three important historical currents: modernism, postmodernism, and pluralism. We live in an era in which the "ideologies of centrism," i.e., the assertion of ethnocentrism, rational-centrism, male-centrism, Eurocentrism, anthropocentrism, and other centrisms, are under scrutiny. It's a good time for inquiring educational dialogues.

James G. Henderson

Endnotes

1. For further discussion of this point, see Henderson, J. G. (1988). A curriculum response to the knowledge base reform movement. *Journal of Teacher Education, 39*(5), 13–17.
2. For a good introduction to the debate in teacher education over the relative merits of a standardized "knowledge base" and of the meaning and value of "technical rationality," see Grimett, P. P., & Erickson, G. L. (Eds.). (1988). *Reflection in teacher education.* New York: Teachers College Press.
3. The constructivist perspective is also argued in the tradition of Piagetian "neo-Kantianism." If you are interested in this philosopical tradition, see Hacker, Peter M. S. (1976). *Insight and illusion: Wittgenstein on philosophy and the metaphysics of experience.* Oxford: Clarendon Press. For Piaget's constructivist argument, see Piaget, J. (1976). *The grasp of consciousness* (S. Wedgwood, Trans.). Cambridge, MA: Harvard University Press. (Original work published 1974.)
4. For a classic statement on the social construction of everyday knowledge, see Berger, P. L., & Luckmann, T. (1966). *The social construction of reality: A treatise in the sociology of knowledge.* New York: Anchor Books/Doubleday.

References

DEWEY, J. (1938). *Experience and education.* New York: Collier.

RORTY, R. (1982). *Consequences of pragmatism.* Minneapolis: University of Minnesota Press.

SCHON, D. A. (1983). *The reflective practitioner: How professionals think in action.* New York: Basic Books.

SCHON, D. A. (1987). *Educating the reflective practitioner: Toward a new design for teaching and learning in the professions.* San Francisco: Jossey-Bass.

Contents

CHAPTER 4

CHAPTER 5

CHAPTER 6

CHAPTER 7

CHAPTER 1

Reflective Teaching and Educational Inquiry

Introduction

The challenge of exemplary teaching is the focus of this book. Although this challenge can be met in various ways, one model of exemplary teaching, the inquiring reflective approach, serves as the framework for this text. You may find that you disagree with this particular model. Keep in mind that it is offered not as *the* answer to teaching excellence, but rather as one of many alternatives. You are welcome, indeed invited, to question it. Throughout the remaining chapters you will read about the recommendations and practices of numerous teachers who have adapted this basic model of inquiring, reflective teaching to their own values, goals, and beliefs. In addition, the text will suggest practical activities to help you develop, test, and refine your own interpretation of this model of teaching excellence.

The Reflective Teacher

Reflective teachers are expert teachers, and they demonstrate their expertise in myriad ways. The most obvious evidence of expert teaching can be found in the classroom. Certainly we expect good teachers to know their subject matter and be able to teach it well. In addition, good teachers must be experts in time management, discipline, psychology, instructional methods, interpersonal communication, and learning theory—and they must practice these competencies under the watchful eyes of 20 to 30 demanding customers.

In *The Practice of Teaching* (1986) Jackson observes that expert teachers "can spot an inattentive student a mile off. They can detect signs of incipient difficulty. Their senses are fully tuned to what is going on around them. They are not easily rattled" (p. 87). Research indicates that teachers make up to 200 major and minor decisions every school day![1] In his now-classic study of teachers, *Life in Classrooms,* (1968), Jackson provides a vivid portrayal of the unrelenting pressure on teachers to respond to problems of all types. Teachers develop confidence and skill in decision making through reflective practice. Reflective teachers willingly embrace their decision-making responsibilities, and they regularly reflect on the consequences of their actions. Maybe they don't solve all of the problems they confront, and maybe they make mistakes, but they never stop trying. They are sincere and thoughtful professionals who constantly learn from their reflective experiences. They understand that receptiveness to further learning is the key to continued professional development and vitality.

The three key characteristics of reflective practice are an *ethic of caring,* a *constructivist approach to teaching,* and *artistic problem solving.*

An Ethic of Caring

The first characteristic of reflective teaching is the ethic of caring, which also serves as the value orientation for this text. Teachers express an ethic of caring through caring thoughtfulness. To care as a teacher is to be ethically bound to understand one's students. Noddings (1984) writes that when a caring "teacher asks a question in class and a student responds, she receives not just the 'response' but the student. What he says matters, whether it is right or wrong, and she probes gently for clarification, interpretation, contribution" (p. 176).

Noddings presents three important, interrelated ways to practice an ethic of caring: *confirmation, dialogue,* and *cooperative practice.* She writes:

> When we attribute the best possible motive consonant with reality to the cared-for, we confirm him; that is, we reveal to him an attainable image of himself that is lovelier than that manifested in his present acts (p. 193).
>
> Confirmation, the loveliest of human functions, depends upon and interacts with dialogue and practice. I cannot confirm a child unless I talk with him and engage in cooperative practice with him (p. 196).

We will explore the values of the ethic of caring by systematically examining the concepts of confirmation, dialogue and cooperative practice.

CONFIRMATION. To confirm a student "we must see the cared-for as he is and as he might be—as he envisions his best self" (Noddings, 1984, p. 67). But what is this "best self"? Clearly it is different for each individual. To become sensitive to the best self of each student, a teacher must take time to listen carefully to each student's innermost yearnings. One student may want to become a mathematician, another an auto mechanic, and a third a writer of Hollywood movie scripts. The caring teacher takes the time to help all students discover their individual inclinations and capitalize on them.

Think of a tracker carefully following an animal's trail. Every telltale sign is important; overlooking a clue may mean losing the quarry. Teachers must track just as carefully to find a student's best self. Along the way they may engage in problem solving, but they must not let this distract them from the intuitive connection they are making.

DIALOGUE. Dialogue is the second important way to practice an ethic of caring. Dialogue guided by an ethic of caring is open to the interplay between feeling and thinking. Think of the closest conversations you've had with a family member or friend. Because you trusted one another, neither of you had to censor what you were saying. You could talk honestly and openly about your innermost concerns. As Noddings notes, the "purpose of dialogue is to come into contact with ideas and to understand, to meet the other and to care" (1984, p. 186).

Caring dialogue between teachers and students is rare in our schools today. Noddings notes that making dialogue a high priority requires two major changes in American schools, one organizational and one cultural. Schools need to reorganize the way they assign pupils to classrooms in order to encourage "extended contact between teachers and students" (p. 186). Of greater significance and difficulty is the need to persuade the American public to accept honest and open communication between students and teachers as an appropriate—and integral—tool of learning.

Some exemplary schools, which you will read about later in this text, have established a flexible, multi-age classroom organization that enables teachers to work with students for up to three years. The benefits of extended teacher-student contact are obvious.

Suppose you are a second-grade teacher who has worked 9 months to build a good working relationship with your students and their parents. You've identified each student's strengths and weaknesses, explored a variety of techniques and approaches to foster each child's best self, and helped them set and accomplish long-term goals. Why pass these children on to a new teacher who will have to build the relationships all over again? Although most children adjust to a new classroom fairly quickly, what about those who have learning disabilities, lack self-confidence, or have difficulty establishing trusting relationships? If your professional opinion tells you that a child would benefit from continuing to work with you, is your school organization flexible enough to accommodate your decision? The same point can be made about high school organization. Why can't teachers work with students for more than 1 semester or 1 year?

The cultural hurdle that impedes caring dialogue in the schools is the commonly held belief that schools should teach technical skills and general abstract knowledge but refrain from discussing values, beliefs, or controversial opinions. In other words, schools should follow the code of conduct of a nice dinner party: the open exchange of ideas is welcome as long as no one brings up religion or politics! Noddings points out that this cultural belief about schools seriously inhibits teachers' ability to establish close relationships with their students. Schools should be "settings in which values, beliefs, and opinions can be examined both critically and appreciatively" (1984, p. 184). Noddings reasons that teachers are already dealing with difficult topics such as racial, cultural, and social diversity; why shouldn't they also deal with diversity of values and beliefs?

COOPERATIVE PRACTICE. Noddings believes that caring teachers must also be "cooperative educators" (p. 186). Teachers guided by an ethic of caring understand that they can't practice personal confirmation and honest dialogue unless they work cooperatively with their students, and perhaps with their students' parents, as well. Caring teachers think of themselves as facilitators of learning; they "act as counselors and advisors in their subject fields and not just as imparters of knowledge" (p. 187).

The Constructivist Approach to Teaching

The second characteristic of reflective teaching is a constructivist approach to teaching. All teachers concern themselves with subject matter, which includes both basic skills and academic content. Reflective teachers emphasize two additional considerations:

1. What is the relationship between what I am trying to teach and my students' past experiences?
2. What is the relationship between what I am trying to teach and my students' personal purposes?

The constructivist theory of learning[2] provides insight into these two reflective questions. Constructivists believe that students are active participants rather than passive recipients during the learning process. In metaphoric terms, students are not just vessels into which the teacher pours knowledge. Instead students are builders of knowledge who actively construct the meaning of their lessons on the foundation of both their past experiences and their personal purposes. For example, a student who is motivated to learn a scientific formula for determining the acceleration of physical bodies actively relates the formal scientific concept of acceleration to her past experiences with how physical objects speed up. An unmotivated student, however, may see no relationship between his own personal interests and experiences and the physics teacher's purposes. This student can be coerced into memorizing the formula, but it may well remain meaningless.[3]

The reflective teacher takes this constructivist perspective and sees learning as a complex interaction among each student's past experiences, personal purposes, and subject matter requirements. This interpretation is diagrammed in Figure 1–1. In putting this theory into practice, reflective teachers strive to relate their subject matter to each student's background, needs and interests. Have you ever experienced teachers who considered your experiences and purposes in teaching their subject? Such teachers didn't ask you to memorize facts and practice rote skills. Instead they found ways to connect the topic to your own life. You will meet two reflective teachers and study their approaches to constructivist teaching in chapter 2.

Artistic Problem Solving

The third characteristic of reflective teaching is artistic problem solving. Teachers who become skilled problem solvers by following an ethic of caring and the constructivist theory of learning provide a special service in their classrooms. They seek ways to make their students' learning

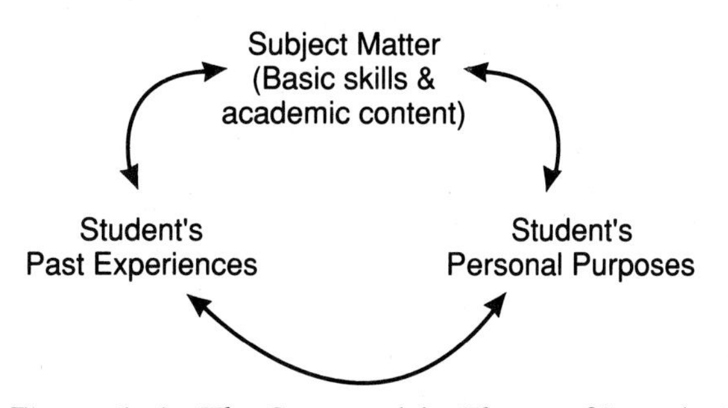

FIGURE 1–1 The Constructivist Theory of Learning.

meaningful by continuously adapting their curriculum to their students' backgrounds, interests, and needs. They understand that quality education involves judgment, imagination, and flexibility. Teaching and learning passivity are not found in the reflective teacher's classroom. Reflective teachers don't ask their students to blindly memorize facts, practice rote skills, and ignore their emotions. Eisner (1985) writes:

> Teaching can be done as badly as anything else. It can be wooden, mechanical, mindless, and wholly unimaginative. But when it is sensitive, intelligent, and creative—those qualities that confer upon it the status of an art—it should, in my view, not be regarded, as it so often is by some, as an expression of unfathomable talent or luck but as an example of humans exercising the highest levels of their intelligence. (p. 177)

Reflective teachers are involved professionals, and they constantly seek new ways to get their students involved. Students discover that the challenges of learning can be aesthetically enjoyable, provocative, and interesting. In later chapters you will encounter specific examples of artistic problem solving.

The Inquiring Educator

Reflective teaching is enhanced by an inquiring attitude toward education. The essence of educational inquiry involves taking a questioning, pondering, democratic perspective on the personal and public virtues of teaching and learning.

Inquiry in the Educational Environment

John Dewey, one of the foremost philosophers in American education, devoted his life to the study of inquiry. He envisioned a highly participative, democratic, educational environment in which people freely raise questions and doubts. In this atmosphere of trust, people may try to persuade but never to manipulate or control one another. They enjoy the process of ethical dialogue, playful exploration, and mutual discovery. Their guiding purpose is to learn from one another through dialogue. Dewey believed that people who experienced an inquiring environment during their formal education would seek ways to establish a democracy based on a "free and enriching communion . . . [in which] social inquiry is indissolubly wedded to the art of free and moving communication" (Dewey, 1927, p. 184).

A Contrast Between Two Educators

A comparison of two teachers' unit plans illustrates the effect of an inquiring approach on reflective teaching. Jack Dusett is a sixth-grade teacher who is teaching a social studies unit on Christopher Columbus' discovery of America. Mr. Dusett is a reflective teacher who wants his students to actively construct their knowledge of Columbus' discovery. To help the students relate the unit to their own experiences and interests, Mr. Dusett asks questions such as these:

- If Christopher Columbus hadn't discovered America in 1492, how might the history of the United States have been different?
- Have you ever discovered something in your neighborhood, such as a new playground, a new movie theater, or a new restaurant? How did this discovery make you feel? How do you think Christopher Columbus felt when he discovered America?

These discussion questions link the subject matter to students' own experiences and make it easier for them to construct their knowledge.

Karen Smiley is also a reflective sixth-grade teacher committed to constructivist learning. But unlike Mr. Dusett, Ms. Smiley is also an inquiring educator. As she plans her unit on Columbus, she looks for materials that help her critically examine the topic. She reads Kirkpatrick Sale's *The Conquest of Paradise: Christopher Columbus and the Columbian Legacy* (1990), which questions Columbus' motives and ecological values. Based on this examination, she decides to include activities that will broaden her students' multicultural perspectives. She shows students a segment of an old cowboy movie in which Native Americans are portrayed as savages. Then she asks students to list adjectives that express how they feel about Native Americans. While teaching the unit, Ms. Smiley will present information from the Native American as well as the European point of view. When the students have completed the unit, she will ask them to make another list of adjectives expressing how they feel about Native Americans. She will analyze and discuss any differences between the two lists with her students.

Ms. Smiley's inquiries aren't limited to the context of her classroom. She has developed an inquiring relationship with several colleagues who enjoy exchanging ideas and evaluating one another's teaching practices. Once or twice a week they gather after school to discuss their experiences. Together they ponder the quality of the classroom leadership and educational service they provide in their respective classrooms. At one of these meetings Ms. Smiley discusses her unit on Columbus. Together they examine the virtues of her curriculum decisions. One colleague arranges to observe several of Ms. Smiley's lessons and shares constructive feedback with the group. All of the teachers look forward to learning new ideas and approaches from these group inquiry experiences.

As you can see, there is a qualitative difference between Jack Dusett and Karen Smiley's reflective teaching. Both teachers are guided by an ethic of caring and the constructivist theory of learning. Ms. Smiley, however, is also deeply committed to educational inquiry, and this commitment influences all of her teaching activities. She constantly seeks opportunities for mutual questioning and discovery—both among her students and among her peers. In fact, she hopes that in time her entire school will become an inquiring community in the spirit of Dewey's vision of a democratic society.

Summary

In this chapter you have been introduced to a model of inquiring, reflective teaching. The key elements of a reflective teacher are an ethic of caring, a constructivist approach to teaching, and artistic problem solving. An inquiring attitude can enhance reflective teaching. Inquiring teachers are eager to question, challenge, and imagine. They seek out opportunities for dialogue with their students, their colleagues, and their society.

Endnotes

1. For a good overview of research on teachers' problem solving, see Clark, C. M., & Peterson, P. L. (1986). Teachers' thought processes. In M. C. Wittrock (Ed.), *Handbook of research on teaching* (3rd ed., pp. 255–296). New York: Macmillan.
2. For a useful overview of constructivist learning research, see Magoon, A. J. (1977). Constructivist approaches to educational research. *Review of Educational Research, 47,* 651–693. For a readable synthesis of constructivist teaching and learning principles, see Fosnot, C. T. (1989). *Enquiring teachers, enquiring learners: A constructivist approach for teaching.* New York: Teachers College Press.
3. For more on constructivist investigations of science learning, see Driver, R., & Bell, B. (1986). Students' thinking and the learning of science: A constructivist view. *School Science Review, 67,* 443–456.

References

DEWEY, J. (1927). *The public and its problems.* New York: Henry Holt.

EISNER, E. W. (1985). *The educational imagination: On the design and evaluation of school programs* (2nd ed.). New York: Macmillan.

JACKSON, P. W. (1968). *Life in classrooms.* New York: Holt, Rinehart & Winston.

JACKSON, P. W. (1986). *The practice of teaching.* New York: Teachers College Press.

NODDINGS, N. (1984). *Caring: A feminine approach to ethics and moral education.* Berkeley, CA: University of California Press.

SALE, K. (1990). *The conquest of paradise: Christopher Columbus and the Columbian legacy.* New York: Knopf.

CHAPTER 2

Two Stories of Reflective Teaching and Educational Inquiry

Introduction

This chapter captures the spirit that infuses the values, beliefs, and ideas of two inquiring educators who exemplify the model of reflective teaching. Although their professional and personal experiences may differ from yours, their aspirations may be similar to your own. Their insights, struggles, dilemmas, reflections, and personalized constructs of education generate a rich, multidimensional portrait of good teaching.

Maura Callahan and Eugene Meyers offered their views on teaching in the form of spoken personal narratives. Although the authentic, unrehearsed, narrative quality of their stories has been preserved, their comments have been loosely organized here around some of the themes that were discussed in chapter 1.

Maura Callahan: Unless It's Me in That Work, What Good Is It?

Maura Callahan has been teaching elementary-school children for 6 years. She began teaching in a Catholic school on the northwest side of Chicago. Later she taught behaviorally disturbed preadolescent boys in an urban residential facility. Now she teaches in a combination learning disability/behavior disorder first-grade classroom. She also coordinates a holistic reading and language arts program for the first through fifth grades.

Building on Her Past Experiences

As a beginning teacher Maura Callahan was unsure of her 6-year-old students' developmental levels and interests. She *was* sure, however, of her own basic philosophy of learning: "Unless it was me in that work, what good is it?" She explains, "Learning is not going to be any fun unless it's about me. And if it's not any fun, it's not going to be worth anything."

Ms. Callahan's philosophy grew out of her own learning experiences. She recalls her elementary school education as dreadful, bleak, and boring. Her teachers were impersonal and distant. "Nobody taught *children,* they taught *subjects* to children," she observes. When Ms. Callahan began teaching she was determined to make a better impression on her own students. From the start she felt a strong sense of identification with them.

> I could have been that child sitting in that classroom. I really wanted to let them know that I was a human being, and I was a kid once too. It's hard to be a kid, and I always told them that.

As a college art student Ms. Callahan had realized that she achieved her best results when she saw a connection between herself and her work. When her work was not tied to her own experiences in some way, she was not motivated to learn. "It would have no meaning for me," she recalls. Today all of her teaching decisions are guided by that one premise, that no matter how old students are or what their abilities, each student must find something of "me"—something of that student's self—in the curriculum.

Confirmation and Dialogue

Ms. Callahan's recollections of her own early school experiences made her sensitive to her students' needs. For example, she remembered that she had difficulty each morning getting focused on school. "I remember myself," she says, "coming from a rather stormy home, the lack of concentration, thinking about what went on at home. I couldn't have cared less about capitalizing the pronoun 'I'."

To ease students' transition from home to school, Ms. Callahan invites them to discuss, privately and in confidence, anything they want to talk about during a daily session she calls "talk time." She knows that addressing students' concerns early in the day enables them to turn their attention more quickly to the tasks at hand. The ritual of talk time sets the stage each day for meaningful student learning. Callahan's caring approach toward her students is a reaction to negative experiences in her own childhood, when teachers talked to her in an intrusive, contrived manner. Today she consciously strives for a positive, supportive, and genuine relationship with her students.

Ms. Callahan believes that focusing on each individual's talents helps students find their own best selves. She and her students often discuss their talents.

> "I think I have talent in art," and, "I did such and such at home," or, "I enjoyed these types of pictures that you showed me." We go at it from that angle. Because they know that's the angle I am stressing in the classroom. Apparently it clicks with them then. They look within themselves to see what their talents are, what they like to do, and what they need to do to get some help to do some more. Budding artists come to talk to me because they know that I was in art before teaching. They think that is really neat, that a teacher who isn't in the art room can draw.

Ms. Callahan tries to help each student in her classroom "to find himself or herself in terms of what they're about, what they're good at, what they can do, and what's important to them." She has never had a set formula for helping students find their best selves. Rather, she encourages them to follow their dreams. She tells them that they can do and have things in life that they may think are not possible.

While helping her students to find their best selves, Ms. Callahan shares her own self with them. She tells them about her experiences as a child and as a commercial artist, about her talents and interests, and about the people who helped her during various stages of her life. By confiding in her students, Ms. Callahan encourages them to confide in her. She hopes her students perceive her as a person whom they can talk to and a person who will really listen.

Constructivist Teaching

In her first year of teaching Ms. Callahan considered various established methods of teaching young children to write, such as rote learning, copying, dictation, and sounding out letters. Guided by her philosophy of "unless it's me in that work, what good is it?" she rejected all of these methods. She chose instead to have her first-grade students write about the babyish things they used to do.

The students generated their own ideas following her examples. Each student gathered ideas, and she helped them with writing and spelling. They learned how to write a rough draft and proofread one another's papers. Using samples from the library, Ms. Callahan showed them different ways to make a book containing their own texts and illustrations.

> They had a vehicle for structure in which they could start to write, plus they could bring in their own experience. Because I felt if we were not talking about ourselves, who would care to write?

Ms. Callahan recalls some of her students' writings: "I used to think babies fell out of the air. I used to think that God was sneezing when there was thunder. I used to think there was a little man in the radio talking." The class delighted in the fact that one idea was funnier than the other. The students were excited about their initial writing experiences because "these were all things that came out of their lives." Ms. Callahan had found a connection between the school's curriculum and each student's self.

Maura Callahan has often had to choose between teaching in a "bookish format" and teaching "within the realm of the world that they know." She steadfastly chose the latter.

> Anything that I ever taught, I've always tried to see what it would mean in terms of their day-to-day life. Because I really don't believe that it would mean anything to them unless it was connected.

The way she accomplishes this is "totally my own way," and never through prepackaged materials. When she teaches rhyming couplets, for example, "there I am with the kids, a hunk of paper, and a bag of markers." Together they create couplets using the students' suggestions. "A lot of it is from their day-to-day lives," Ms. Callahan notes, "and that's that."

As a reflective teacher Ms. Callahan relates subject matter to her students' experiences, needs, and interests. In her fifth-grade language arts class she draws on her students' familiarity with commercial advertising to teach persuasive writing techniques. First she asks students to list their favorite television commercials. She selects a few examples to analyze with the class. Ms. Callahan describes their reaction:

> It's a very interesting experience, because they are extremely enthusiastic about this. We talk about what it actually means to persuade somebody to do something. I have them bring in the ads because this is one of the most obvious forms of persuasion. I have them think about how you explain to your mother why you need to buy a certain thing, or why she should drive you to a baseball game. What you're trying to do is to change somebody's mind. They actually analyze their own kind of strategies in conversations that way. Then I say, "How would you like to make your own commercial?" They get very excited, because this is one thing they've never done.

Ms. Callahan encourages her students to create an innovative product of their own. Students analyze and carry out all the steps of a presentation to make people want the product. They write scripts and work out illustrations. Then Ms. Callahan guides them in putting it all together. They deliver the presentation themselves, on tape, so they learn about voice, inflection, and how to address a group. "We end up with the most wonderful back-to-back ads show that you would ever want to see," declares Ms. Callahan.

To judge the effectiveness of her methods, Ms. Callahan observes students' reactions in class. Her class is always noisy, filled with laughter and fun. It is loud "with a purpose," she explains. "I'm always looking for something I can make their own."

> I used to see in our reading lab situations with teachers who are very much by the book and for the book. The kids used to sit there like bumps on a log. Get somebody with a more creative bent, who could connect the learning experience to the kids' real lives, and you'd have the same kids literally jumping on desks—

> much to the chagrin of those other teachers, who would complain about the noise. But that's how I've always judged it.

Ms. Callahan makes a distinction between teaching methods that are both fun and meaningful and those that involve "pulling a rabbit out of a hat," or fun that does not sustain any meaningful learning. Examples of the latter include such activities as work sheets or games that keep kids busy but don't help them learn.

> I've seen children dance, clap, and jump up and down with teachers who pull rabbits out of hats. Those are the types of lessons and experiences in school that may be fun for awhile, but it's nothing that continues on, or really reaches anything in a meaningful way.

Ms. Callahan notes that many new teachers have learned plenty of "rabbit out of the hat techniques" in their methods classes. She suggests that teachers need to evaluate the purpose of such activities before using them.

Artistic Problem Solving

Her 6 years of teaching have not been without challenges. Ms. Callahan recalls Mark, her first learning disabled student to be mainstreamed for reading. Even though he did well in the reading group, he would return to class emotionally drained, and he sometimes became violent. Ms. Callahan spoke to the reading teacher and to Mark, but was unable to identify the problem. She then contacted Mark's mother, who described Mark's unusual behavior at home. Every morning Mark would stare at himself in the bathroom mirror and say he hated school. His appetite was decreasing, and his temper tantrums at home were growing more frequent.

On the basis of what she had learned Ms. Callahan decided to take a low-key approach at school. One day when she found Mark hitting another student during recess, Ms. Callahan embraced him and said, "I know that you're really hurting inside, Mark. Something is bothering you, and I'm not sure what it is." She continued this supportive, nonjudgmental approach and consulted frequently with Mark's mother. Eventually they discovered that Mark was upset because students in the mainstream class had ridiculed him for his weight and his clumsiness in gym class. Mark feared he would never have any friends in the new classroom.

Relieved that students were not stigmatizing him because of his learning disabilities, Ms. Callahan continued to offer Mark her support. She helped him realize that his violent reactions would not make students like him better. In time, Mark was able to make friends in the new class. Once he knew that his classmates really did care about him, his aggressive behaviors ceased.

A less caring teacher might have handled this situation quite differently. Instead of looking for the cause of Mark's problem, she might have punished him for the symptom—aggressive behavior—and ostracized him even further. Perhaps the situation would have culminated in Mark's removal from the mainstream class. Such disciplinary action would have been easy and convenient for the teacher, but it would have been a serious disservice to Mark. Instead Ms. Callahan gathered information, reflected on the situation, and made the decision to support her student in overcoming his problem and moving one step closer to his own best self.

Cooperative Practice

Ms. Callahan encourages strong parent-teacher relationships, a practice she established during her early years in the Catholic school. "Having the interaction with parents, and trying to look at children holistically, was second nature to me, because this is what happens in a private school." The parents wanted their children to be there, and many made financial sacrifices to enable them to attend that school. Teachers and parents shared the common goal of educating the children. In the public school, some colleagues found Ms. Callahan's focus on parent-teacher relationships unusual.

> But looking at the children and their needs, I realized immediately that I couldn't do this job without the help of all of those parents. Most of the kids came from single-parent homes. I got to know a lot about what went on out of school. I knew there was no way that school could mean anything unless we were all in this together.

Keeping in touch with students' parents is not easy. Ms. Callahan often stays at school until 6:00 p.m. and invites parents for informal meetings.

She is convinced that the extra effort is worth it. With parents' cooperation, she believes, any problem can be resolved.

> I tell the parents, "You're here and I'm here, we can work this out. We can do it." It requires getting to know the parents and building a trusting relationship with them.

Ms. Callahan noted that parents' eagerness to provide the best for their children sometimes seems to backfire. Numerous parents hold second jobs to help pay for music lessons, sports equipment, fashionable clothes, and the like. With all the activities and jobs, however, some families never have the time to eat a meal together. Families are physically and emotionally fragmented, and some kids have no one whom they feel they can really confide in. In addition, Ms. Callahan worries that constant shuttling among organized activities stifles students' natural creativity.

> Sure, they might be learning how to dance or swim, but I think they are learning how *not* to have one imaginative bone in their bodies, or to dream, or to just sit and watch a cloud go by like I used to do. I think the shuttling kind of dulls their ability to get in touch with that creative part of themselves.

Students are so accustomed to structure and organization that they are unable to respond creatively when no structure is provided. Instead they express boredom and a desire to be entertained. Fortunately, Ms. Callahan was surprised to discover, it is not difficult to stimulate their imaginations.

> I think everything I do and the way that I do it is so different from anything they have seen in a schoolroom that I am very appealing to them. With young children, if they like the teacher, they'll go along with you. Once they're in your power you can turn them on to the power within themselves.

Eventually students carry their excitement about classroom learning to their out-of-school lives. They begin to talk about school with enthusiasm and share their schoolwork with their parents. In turn, parents visit the classroom to see why their children are so excited about school.

Setting and Achieving Personal-Professional Goals

How did Ms. Callahan develop the agility to meet administrative criteria without sacrificing her own teaching values and philosophy? She feels that confidence in herself and her goals was the key.

> I know I am a good teacher, and I'm confident about what I'm doing. If the principal walks into my room, I am able to explain the rationale for what I am doing. I'm not fearful. I'm not fearful because I believe in my teaching, and I believe that I can provide a rationale that in some way will be compatible with the objectives of the district.

She admits that this confidence is not handed out along with your degree. It requires hard work, careful self-evaluation, and a willingness to adapt. Unfortunately many pre-service teacher education programs fail to provide students an opportunity for reflection. She advocates a more diversified approach.

> We may have to throw out the teacher manual and look for each person's "raw material." We need to recognize that the people involved are the primary source, not some book. A strong sense of reflection within one's own experiences, within one's own curriculum, is what brings a person to the realization that "unless I am in this, it's not going to have any significant value to me at all." If anything is really going to stick or take place or have an effect, then it has to come from within. That's a belief a teacher must have. And unless that belief is conscious, there will be no evidence of it in practice.

The structure of many educational institutions does not encourage reflection. Instead, Ms. Callahan notes, the institutions require people to play games—"games within the classrooms at school, games to obtain credentials, and games to satisfy the expectations of the district." Having to play such games clouds a person's own philosophy.

> We waltz around in this cloud of denial, in this cloud of artificiality that is not as passive a thing as we think it is. It's destroying the chance to really speak the truth, and to identify the problem, as we pretend that it doesn't exist.

Ms. Callahan strives for a return to reality. "I think that more kids can be reached by getting down to the nuts and bolts. . . . to what really is going to matter, what really is going to last when we learn anything in life." In many school districts, however, teachers are expected to simply follow the philosophy imposed from above rather than their own. In Harry Wolcott's (1973) book *The Man in the Principal's Office* he states, "There are no individual philosophies in a school district, there is only one [top-down] philosophy, the rest are merely attitudes."

> When a teacher's own philosophy, which I believe should be the guiding force, is reduced to a mere attitude, we have a very serious problem. I've seen many good teachers put to death by an attitude. When I read that statement, it occurred to me that our organized learning attempt has been, in a sense, our own death warrant.

When teachers who know what students are interested in and would like to learn instead pursue something else, both teachers and students end up leading a double life. Ms. Callahan adamantly refuses to do this. She attributes her success as a teacher to her philosophy of "always striving for the reality to come through" in her classroom.

Eugene Meyers: Celebrating Students, Friends for Life

Eugene Meyers is a veteran of 21 years of teaching. He taught for 10 years in primarily black schools in Chicago. Eleven years ago he was reassigned to his current location, a racially balanced school in an integrated area. Mr. Meyers teaches English to academically talented seventh- and eighth-grade students. He also teaches independent studies in literature and creative writing to juniors and seniors.

Constructing Personal-Professional Knowledge

Unlike Maura Callahan, who conscientiously applied her insights about her own learning to her teaching, Eugene Meyers began teaching without a clear idea of the type of teacher he wanted to become. At first, he recalls, his greatest concern was maintaining control of the class.

> I always used to think my options were either to have everyone sitting behind a desk or to have Cuisenaire rods flying all over the place. Later I learned there was a way for me to have sufficient control over the dynamics to be able to go where I wanted to go and teach my students in a much more real way.

He was inspired by visions of caring teaching portrayed in movies and books from the 1960s, such as Sidney Poitier's character in *To Sir With Love*. But he quickly discovered that it was impossible to emulate someone else's *style* of teaching. "You can't be somebody else," he says. What you can do, however, is work on developing your own personal teaching qualities, values, and beliefs.

Eugene Meyers struggled with the same issues you are most likely to struggle with, such as developing successful problem-solving, curriculum, and classroom management strategies. He began his teaching career with the standard knowledge of educational theory and methods, as well as his own romanticized images of teaching. Through his classroom experiences and interactions with other teachers, Mr. Meyers began to develop approaches that worked well for him. He constructed his own personal-professional knowledge as he went; this developmental process was slow and difficult. Looking back he observes, "Teaching is a wonderful profession, but no way is it easy. You have to decide what kind of teacher you want to be, and then you have to work at it."

Mr. Meyers' teaching strategies evolved over a 20-year period. For example, in his early teaching years Mr. Meyers randomly gave various kinds of assignments. Some of them worked, and some did not. He began to notice that certain kinds of assignments were more effective than others. He also noticed that his observations about effective assignments could help him find better ways to achieve academic goals.

> It struck me that, just as I liked to talk about myself, students get most involved when they're talking about themselves. Writing makes one feel very vulnerable. The more involved the writer is in the writing, the more willing he or she is to tolerate that vulnerability.

Constructivist Teaching

Although Mr. Meyers sets traditional academic goals for his students, he achieves those goals by integrating his students' life experiences into the classroom. He concluded long ago that if school is separated from a child's life, it is pointless.

> I think the reason schooling sometimes seems irrelevant to students is no one shows them its integration. The more we can integrate school and the real world, the more learning will actually get inside them. Through subject matter we're helping them actualize themselves. If drawing on these other aspects of their lives helps them get the skills they need, then they should bring those aspects into the classroom. We have to provide them with avenues to bring them into the classroom.

For example, he teaches grammar in a practical, problem-solving way. Students bring in what they perceive as awkward sentences or grammatical errors from newspapers, television, or radio. They then justify their perceptions using examples from their own writing or outside sources.

Such integration must take place within academic areas, as well. Rather than teach the traditional components of English as separate strands, Mr. Meyers combines them to show the interrelationships among grammar, writing, and literature. For example, he uses a writing assignment to help students grasp the literary concept of point of view. First students retell a familiar fairy tale from a third-person point of view. Then students rewrite it as an autobiographical story from a first-person point of view. Students experience firsthand the strengths and limitations of narrative perspective. They also begin to develop an appreciation of psychological elements such as emotional distance. Knowing how language works in certain situations allows students to read in a more involved way. And involved readers usually become lifelong readers.

Teacher's and Students' Personal Purposes

Reading, discussing, and writing about literature have another benefit.

> English is a subject that asks us what it means to be human. If it's taught well, it's a very inviting subject. It asks us what it means to be alive, to be ourselves. It allows us to freely talk about things like our fear of death, our fear of falling in love, the confusion of being in love, in the context of *Hamlet* or *Romeo and Juliet.* In one sense it becomes very risky when you're writing about it, but in another sense it's kind of protective, because you're talking about yourself through other people.

Creative writing offers students another opportunity to talk about themselves. Mr. Meyers emphasizes to his students that they create an atmosphere out of their own experiences. "You're the god of your own story," he tells them. They write for themselves and for each other, not just to complete a classroom assignment.

Although his students may not love English, he is confident that they feel closer to it because they approach it through their own life experiences. "If you give students assignments that let them talk about themselves," he explains, "the kids feel more of a commitment to the assignment, to you, and to what you're teaching."

Encouraging students to express their ideas about what they read helps them become lifelong readers. "They talk about ideas," he says, "because I make ideas exciting to talk about." *Hamlet,* for example, is not a work most teenagers come to eagerly, but he enables them to see something of themselves in the protagonist. Mr. Meyers recalls a discussion about Hamlet believing in the idea of providence and of God. One student turned to him and asked plaintively, "Well, do you believe in them?"

> I think he didn't want Hamlet to have such an easy answer, because he himself didn't believe in it. I said to him, "No, I don't. I'm not that happy a person that I think there's a future that God has planned out. I don't see life as that organized and that wonderful, but I'd be very happy if I did." I thought it was lovely that he was able to ask me that in that kind of a voice. This kid was really thinking, "Gee, I hope that there's somebody out there who's as hopelessly lost as I am." And of course I was. So it was a relief for him.

Educational Inquiry

To enrich his teaching Mr. Meyers turns to his own interests in literature, music, art, and theater for inspiration. He designed a course, for example, that focuses on how literary patterns change in different media. Students study a literary work that has been made into a movie, television program, ballet, opera, or symphony. The students themselves are a great resource as well.

> The kind of energy and experiences and information that students bring is phenomenal. If you were to read the stories . . . their knowledge of material that is not taught in school, cultural things, like life in other countries, what it's like to be a

> dancer, what it's like to play the harp. I don't mean naturally be good at baseball and pick up a team. Their sense of commitment to activity is more extensive than most children I've taught elsewhere, because they have experienced the emotional commitment to doing something over an extended period of time. Whether it's a ballet class or swim team or choir, they're more in touch with their own emotions. I think they tend to understand literature better, and in their own writing they portray emotions more vividly.

Artistic Problem Solving

Most students like the teacher more than the subject matter, Mr. Meyers suspects. "If you knew that your teacher cared about you, you would like his class, and him." Occasionally he encounters a student who does not easily accept him or the class. A youngster in his class a few years ago was afraid to participate in class discussions, but did average work on his individual written assignments. He couldn't talk about himself aloud, but he began to do so through his writing. Mr. Meyers' acceptance and support enabled this student to express in writing his feelings about a literary work. In turn, this student had a profound influence on Mr. Meyers.

> More than any student I've ever had, this was *my* child. I really seemed to have nurtured something good, something important in him. There's more to the world than just math and science, and I mean math and science as a metaphor for this sort of tight world of rules. One of my best experiences was with this kid.

Mr. Meyers continues to help those students who are more vulnerable bring something of themselves into their work. "They sometimes don't do it exactly the way you would expect them to, or the way everyone else does, but they do it, in their own way," he said.

Caring

As a veteran teacher Mr. Meyers continues to reflect on how he interacts with his students. He concludes, "I do a lot of metaphorical sort of hugging with the kids." When students leave his class, he hopes they take away more than just an appreciation of literature.

> I think they also take away the feeling that I really care about them. I really hope they learn something about English. I think they do. I think they also learn something about ideas, that ideas are exciting, and thinking about ideas is exciting.

Mr. Meyers thinks that being a friend to your students is worth the effort it takes to cultivate that friendship while maintaining mutual respect.

> Through reflection I discovered how much my students mean to me, as people. I spend my entire day with them. I have an investment in believing that my students are valuable, because my closest co-workers in this process are the children. The relationship you have with your students is yours alone. The 9 months you share can be an intimate, unique, and caring experience. Sometimes children feel frustrated, there's tension, and disagreement, but my kids know that I love them. And I love them educationally, constructively, and by trying to help them become more successful learners. My students know when they leave my class that they have a friend for life.

Service

It is a mistake, Mr. Meyers believes, to reward teachers professionally and monetarily by moving them into nonteaching, administrative positions. Although he's certain he would be a good administrator, he would rather devote his life to teaching. He also believes veteran teachers should contribute to the profession by mentoring novice teachers.

> Mentoring allows people who come out of the university to have somebody there to help them with the whole process of acculturation into a school. It also allows the veteran teachers to have contact with the university. They can be involved in making the study of the process of education better.

In particular Mr. Meyers wants to help beginning teachers develop child-centered classrooms, in which children are involved in both the curriculum and the process of education.

> Some teachers think it's okay to throw in some occasional student participation, just a few crumbs. What I'm saying is that the student has to be fully integrated into the process, even into the goals of the process. I teach English, and my goals are English goals. But I know that my students want to communicate effectively. Once they admit that they want to communicate effectively, I try to suggest ways in which they can do that. But they start out by believing in *their* goal, and they're involved in the process. That's the only way they're going to learn anything.

Getting more schools to practice child-centered education is difficult. Institutions want to maintain the status quo, teachers believe what they are doing is adequate, and boards of education mistakenly think educational reform must mean more money and smaller classes. "They have to think about student involvement in the classroom and in their own education," Mr. Meyers contends. Teachers must make students' education an integral part of their lives, not something that's separate from their real world.

Think about why you want to become an educator, Mr. Meyers suggests. Education is exciting, joyful, and fulfilling. Too many people enter the field of education for the wrong reasons. When they encounter bright students who are excited, they think the students are being unruly, or talking back, or getting off task. To be a good teacher, Mr. Meyers believes, you have to be excited about education.

Summary

Maura Callahan and Eugene Meyers exemplify the inquiring, reflective teaching model introduced in chapter 1. Both teachers fit Noddings' (1984) description of the caring teacher: They take the time to dialogue with their students, they work cooperatively with them, and they help each individual discover his or her best self. Eugene Meyers' description of how he teaches the concept of point of view and Maura Callahan's technique for teaching persuasive writing are examples of applied constructivist learning theory. When problems arise in the classroom, these teachers invest the time and energy necessary to find the solution that is best for the student, not just for themselves. Finally, both teachers are questioning, challenging, probing individuals who seek personal and professional growth for themselves and intellectual, emotional, and social growth for their students through the process of inquiry.

Personal-Professional Inquiry

Maura Callahan believes that teachers can begin to become good teachers by "coming to this themselves through a very keen and guided sense of reflection." The following questions will further your personal-professional inquiry.

1. Consider the beliefs Ms. Callahan held during her first year of teaching: "Learning is not going to be any fun unless it's about me. And if it's not any fun, it's not going to be worth anything." As a student who will soon become a teacher, what beliefs do you hold about teaching?
2. Early in her teaching career Ms. Callahan had to choose to either follow a "bookish format" or teach her own way by connecting subject matter with her students' experiences. What did she choose and why? If faced with a similar situation, what would you choose to do? What factors might influence your decision?
3. Mr. Meyers thinks that to be a good teacher you must be excited about education. Do you agree or disagree? Why? Why do you want to be a teacher?
4. Mr. Meyers believes that some experienced teachers are afraid to give up control because they think it will result in chaos. How do you view the issue of control? How will you respond to a student whose behavior is interpreted as passive and withdrawn? How will you respond to a student whose behavior is interpreted as aggressive, rebellious, and disruptive?
5. What is your reaction to Ms. Callahan's statement that "our organized learning attempt has been our own death warrant"?
6. Both Ms. Callahan and Mr. Meyers have become reflective teachers through personally unique developmental processes. They both have academic goals and believe in reaching these goals by connecting subject matter with students' needs, interests, and experiences. Do you think you can grow into a reflective teacher? Why or why not? What factors might promote or hinder your development as a reflective teacher?

References

NODDINGS, N. (1984). *Caring: A feminine approach to ethics and moral education.* Berkeley, CA: University of California Press.

WOLCOTT, H. (1973). *The man in the principal's office.* New York: Holt, Rinehart & Winston.

CHAPTER 3

Preparing for Constructivist Learning:

BECOMING A STUDENT OF YOUR OWN TEACHING

Introduction

In chapter 2 you discovered how two teachers adapted the model of an inquiring, reflective educator to their own needs, goals, values, and beliefs. Perhaps you encountered a glimpse of yourself in their stories; perhaps you felt that neither teacher has much to offer you. Remember that these teachers serve only as examples of a model that can be implemented in myriad ways. Bringing your own version of this model to life, and allowing it to grow and change as you grow and change, is the challenging task before you.

In the process of becoming a teacher you are being barraged with a seemingly endless presentation of ideas, methods, philosophies, terminologies, theories, generalizations, recommendations, etc. You surely have realized by now that no two authorities—whether they be teachers, researchers, or education professors—totally agree on all aspects of the art and science of teaching. But most would probably agree on one point: Each teacher needs to find the unique combination of ideas, methods, and philosophies that works best for him or her.

You don't need to wait until you have your own classroom to begin to become the best teacher you can be. You can start now, by becoming an inquiring, reflective student. Applying what you have learned to yourself as a student has both a professional and a personal purpose. It gives you, a future reflective teacher, insight into how to facilitate meaningful learning for your students. On a personal level it provides the constructivist link between the formal content matter of the text and your own experiences and purposes.

Reflective Practice

As you recall, the three essential elements of the reflective teaching model are the ethic of caring, the constructivist theory of learning, and artistic problem solving. Let's examine how you can incorporate these elements into the way you deal with yourself as a student.

Caring for Yourself

You can't practice an ethic of caring if you don't care for yourself. Noddings (1984) wrote: "An ethic of caring is a tough ethic. It does not separate self and other in caring. . . . If caring is to be maintained, clearly, the one-caring must be maintained" (pp. 99–100). Abbs (1981) describes the importance of self-regard in teaching: "Before you can teach well, you must be a self-sustaining individual with your own alert life" (p. 122). You can practice the ethic of caring on yourself using the same techniques good teachers use with their students: confirmation and dialogue.

CONFIRMATION. Confirming yourself, or becoming sensitive to your own best self, requires that you take the time to listen to a deeper part of yourself that is not controlled by the analytical habits you have developed as a member of a modern society. Finding your best self is more a poetic embrace than an analytical triumph. Your best self may reveal itself through intuition and metaphor. Abbs (1981) writes that using metaphor is "a unique and enduring and irreplaceable way of embodying the truths of our inward lives" (p. 119). Later in this chapter you will practice specific techniques for discovering your own personal metaphors.

Although personal confirmation is a celebration of individuality, it is an individuality grounded in a sense of positive freedom—the understanding that individual rights are exercised in the context of community responsibilities. Our best selves are always directed toward positive contributions, not negative ones. Actions that profit oneself at the expense of others are individualistic, but they do not originate from a best-self orientation. For example, a student who tears an important article out of a journal at the library may receive a better grade on a term paper than those students who were unable to read the missing pages. This is an individualistic action motivated by selfishness, insensitivity, or greed. It does not originate from a best-self orientation.

The motivations of our best selves are virtuous. Our best selves are sensitive to connectedness and directed toward making positive contributions. As a teacher your best self will strive to contribute to the interdependent social environment of your classroom, your school, and your community. Clearly there are many unique and creative ways to do this.

Unfortunately (or perhaps fortunately), a best-self orientation in teaching is not as readily apparent as this discussion implies. The term *best self* is interpretive. Different people will have different ideas as to how to contribute positively to a school's interdependent environment. For example, suppose you are the faculty advisor for the student newspaper. A student writes an article on teenage pregnancy that features several students who are pregnant. Should you allow this student to print the article? The article may be well written and may raise school awareness on a timely topic, but what if it causes pain to the students who are featured? What if the article leads some parents to call for increased censorship of student publications? What if the potential controversy might put your job at risk?

How would your teaching best self respond to these questions? Do your peers agree with you? Can't good teachers who have differing interpretations of their best selves disagree on the best course of action in this situation?

DIALOGUE. Dialogue is the second important way to practice an ethic of caring. Just as teachers must be careful to use fair and just language with their students, you must be careful to use fair and just language with yourself. Positive self-dialogue or self-affirming contemplation—the manner in which you reflect—can have considerable impact on your motivation, confidence, and success.

For example, what do you say to yourself when things don't go the way you planned or hoped? Do you dwell on the disappointments, or do you look for positive aspects of a situation? Do you take concrete steps to make future endeavors more successful by pinpointing problems and possible solutions, or do you simply blame yourself for being incompetent or unlucky? Do you analyze what *you* did right and wrong, or do you assume that other people were responsible for the disappointing outcome? How you talk to yourself after a disappointment or a success helps determine whether you learn from your experiences in constructive ways or simply distort your world view to protect your own ego.

Creatively Constructing Your Own Knowledge

Perhaps you have already heard or read about a particular kind of teaching that you know is not suitable for you. Can you explain why it is unsuitable? Maybe you have observed methods that you think might work well. How can you be sure about them? Can you list the goals, values, or principles you think will be most important to you when you have your own classroom?

As you recall from chapter 1 the constructivist theory of learning holds that students acquire new knowledge by relating it to their past experiences and to their personal purposes. If you apply this theory to yourself as a student of education, you will find that examining your experiences and purposes will help you to critically evaluate the various philosophies and methods you encounter in terms of your own goals, values, and principles. Taking such a reflective approach allows you to focus your attention on those ideas that are most appropriate for you as a future teacher.

As a reflective student you need to ask yourself two questions.

1. What is the relationship between what I am trying to learn and my own past experiences?
2. What is the relationship between what I am trying to learn and my personal purposes?

To facilitate answering these questions you must first identify key experiences that may have influenced your perception of the education process. These key experiences may, in turn, help to explain why certain purposes are most significant for you as a future teacher. These purposes are also closely related to your vision of your own best self.

Perhaps you are unsure just how to determine what past experiences may help you in becoming a good teacher. If so, you may find it useful to explore your remembered anecdotes, role models, and personal metaphors.

Remembered Anecdotes and Role Models. Remembered anecdotes, both positive and negative, serve as influential experiential referents for our learning constructions. For example, you may recall how you struggled with a particular concept in school until your teacher finally hit upon a new approach that made everything clear. On the other hand, perhaps you have a negative feeling about a certain subject because your teacher's method of presenting it was dull and tiresome. Such anecdotes, and the feelings they evoke in you, may have a strong influence over how you would approach a similar situation when you are a teacher.

Similarly, the social learning we acquire from observing significant role models is also an influential referent in later learning. We often aspire to be like those people whom we admire. Identifying those people who were or are role models in your life helps you clarify what goals you will set for yourself.

PERSONAL METAPHORS. The personal metaphors we use to describe teaching are another important influence on our learning constructions. You may not be as familiar with this concept as you are with the ideas of remembered anecdotes and role models, so this topic of exploration will be explained in more detail.

Imagine the following lunchroom conversation among four teachers over how they feel about teaching:

Ken: For me, teaching is a battle between an adult and a group of captive, restless children.

Janis: I think that's too harsh an image. For me, teaching is like a roller-coaster ride with lots of ups and downs.

Connie: I like that theme park imagery, but I prefer to think of teaching as riding a merry-go-round. The ride can be pleasant, with lovely music. Then, all of a sudden, you become dizzy from the swirl of motion and emotion. The music turns to noise. Confusion! Chaos! It's exhausting.

Bob: I wish I could relax more when I teach. I'm so wound up at the end of a school day—just like a top ready to spin out of control. You know, I feel like I always have to maintain control. I'm like the Dutch boy who had to keep his thumb in the dike to prevent a flood.

Ken: . . . or a battle. That's why I think of teaching as warfare. If you aren't careful, the enemy forces will overwhelm you.

Bob: I don't know about this warfare business. Sometimes I think I should just pull my thumb from the dike. Maybe instead of being caught in a flood, I'll feel like Huck Finn rafting down the Mississippi River on a soft summer day.

Janis: The sense of a ride. I'd agree with that. Kind of like a feather floating in the breeze. Or is it more like a raft crashing through a river rapids? Maybe it's both!

Connie: I think teaching is more like a dance. When the music isn't too jarring, you can get into some neat rhythms with the kids. Anyone for a tango?

Ken: Very funny! There's the bell. Battle stations, everyone!

Janis: Ken, I wish you could have a different experience in the classroom. If you imagined teaching differently, maybe you could see other sides to your work.

These teachers are revealing their feelings about teaching through personal metaphors. A metaphor describes one thing in terms of another. Teaching is not literally a "battle" or a "roller-coaster ride," but such images effectively convey a particular sense the teachers have about their work. When we use metaphors, we "exploit the power of connotation and analogy [that] awakens our senses" (Eisner, 1985, p. 226).

Elbaz (1981) describes metaphors as a combination of a "teacher's feelings, values, needs, and beliefs" (p. 61). She adds that a teacher's metaphor "is generally imbued with a judgment of value and constitutes a guide to the intuitive realization of the teacher's purposes" (p. 61). Elbaz cites the example of Sarah, a high school English teacher whose personal metaphors she analyzed. "Sarah wanted 'to have a *window* onto the kids and what they're thinking,' and, in turn, she wanted her own *window* to be more open" (p. 62).

Connelly and Clandinin (1985) discovered that teachers have a rich repertoire of "personal practical knowledge composed of such experiential matters as images, rituals, habits, cycles, routines, and rhythms" (pp. 194–195). They describe a primary-grade teacher who makes gingerbread cookies with her students. This teacher imagines her classroom as "home" (p. 188). Think a minute about that metaphor. What feelings does it evoke in you? Did you have a teacher who gave you a sense of the classroom as home?

In chapter 2 you read about two teachers whose values and beliefs about teaching are apparent in their personal metaphors. When Maura Callahan talked about learning, she used the metaphor of *getting down to the nuts and bolts*:

> I think that more kids can be reached by getting down to the nuts and bolts. Rip it all out, gut it all out, that's my metaphor. Get down to what really is going to matter, what really is going to last when we learn anything in life.

To Maura Callahan, *getting down to the nuts and bolts* meant helping each student discover his or her own self. Do you recall Eugene Meyers' reference to his students as *co-workers*? He used this image in the following way: "I have an investment in believing that my students are valuable, because my closest co-workers in this process are the children." To Eugene Meyers, treating students as co-workers meant respecting them as people, and valuing the experiences they bring to school.

You have collected both positive and negative metaphors on teaching from past experiences as a teacher or from your many years as a student. Two strategies will help you discover the personal metaphors you hold about teaching. They are called *clustering* and *expressive writing*.

Clustering. Clustering is a "brainstorming process akin to free association" (Rico, 1983, p. 28). Rico developed clustering to help people evoke "the mental life of daydream, random thought, remembered incident, image, or sensation" (p. 28). Figure 3–1 is an example of a cluster created around the nuclear phrase "inquiring, reflective teacher." Clustering can help you identify the ways you express your feelings about teaching. Think back to the four teachers' lunchroom conversation. They were expressing metaphorically how they felt about teaching. Clustering can help you do the same.

To practice clustering, follow these steps. Set aside some quiet time so that you can listen carefully to your thoughts. Write down a "nucleus" (Rico, 1983) phrase or word in the middle of a sheet of paper. Then freely associate around this nucleus. Write all of the words and phrases you think of around the central term. Circle these associations and draw lines between the expressions that you feel are closely related. You may want to add arrows to the lines to indicate the direction of the connection. Continue to cluster for several minutes until you feel you have run out of ideas.[1]

After creating your cluster, examine it for personal metaphors—for all of the analogies and images that express how you feel. Once you have identified the personal metaphors in your cluster, ask yourself several related questions. Do these metaphors serve me well? Am I happy with the way I have expressed myself? Are my images of teaching too limited? Could I become more evocative, more poetically aware? Do I need to consider Janis' advice to Ken: "Maybe, if you imagined teaching differently, you could see other sides to your work"?

If you are satisfied with your personal expressions on teaching, you may feel no desire to respond to these questions. If you are not satisfied or if you are just feeling curious, you may want to explore new metaphors. New metaphors can "reveal a truth about the world we had not previously recognized" (Rico, 1983, p. 187). Cassirer (1946) argues that when we create new symbols and images we become "aesthetically liberated" (p. 98).

Expressive Writing. If you are concerned about your "aesthetic liberation," you may benefit from expressive writing. Begin by reviewing the personal metaphors in your cluster. Select one or more of these images and compose a brief essay that expands on the metaphoric theme or themes you have selected. For example, the student who created the cluster in Figure 3–1 composed the following expressive paragraph on two of her images: "teachers as explorers" and "teachers as investigative reporters":

✱ An inquiring, reflective teacher is an explorer, not of outer space, but of inner space. In the quest for teaching excellence, she is willing to venture into uncharted territory, and does not let the fear of failure daunt her efforts to solve students' problems by trying to see them in a

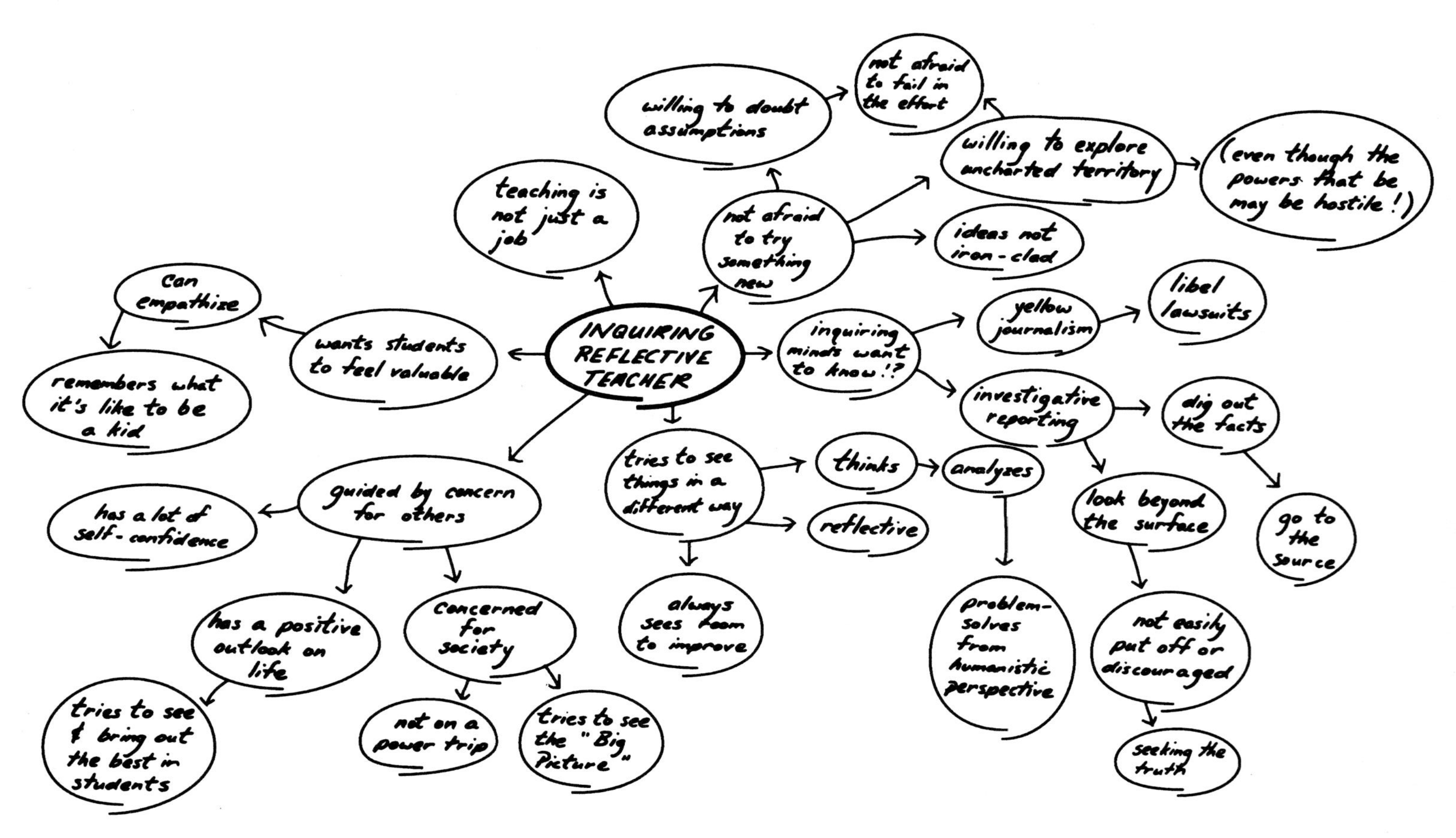

Figure 3–1 A Cluster Around the Nuclear Phrase "Inquiring Reflective Teacher."

> new way, or look at them from different points of view. Because this teacher operates out of an ethic of caring and concern for students and the society they are preparing to join, her ultimate goal is to build their self-esteem and increase learning by making school a positive experience. Like an investigative reporter, an inquiring, reflective teacher looks beyond the surface, rejecting easy labels put onto problems, and instead tries to dig out the facts and get to the source of the difficulty.

Once you have completed your expressive essay (or essays), ponder these questions. Could you expand further on any of your personal images? Do you need to consider other images of teaching?

Inquiry

Inquiring teachers think about the virtues of their activities. Karen Smiley designed activities that encourage critical thinking about Christopher Columbus because she believes that the ability to consider more than one viewpoint on an issue is valuable both to her students and to society as a whole. Thus her teaching activities reflect her contributive values and her firm belief in the value of inquiring discourse.

Contributive Inquiry

To review an important point, a best-self orientation is grounded in contributive values. With these values we are motivated to help create "public spaces" where people can act "in concert" (Greene, 1988). There are at least three community referents for teachers' contributive inquiries: national, institutional, and classroom.

The National Community Referent. This text advocates certain values that nationally (and perhaps internationally) bind many professional educators together. Consider for a moment some of the major value positions you have already encountered in the book:

1. Expert teachers are active problem solvers.
2. An ethic of caring is an important dimension of constructivist teaching.
3. Caring teachers inquire broadly.
4. Historical awareness provides perspective on the common sense referents to "good" teaching.

These values are shared by many members of the national professional community. Do you share some or all of these positions? How will your constructivist efforts contribute to a national community of professional educators?

As you consider this question (as well as the other inquiries in this section), the distinction between *contribution* and *conformity* is quite pertinent. Contributing to a community does not mean simply conforming to its current values without reflection. Some of the most important contributors to our present society have challenged current values to bring about justice. Martin Luther King, for example, challenged the existing social and political structure to obtain racial equality.

THE INSTITUTIONAL COMMUNITY REFERENT. The institutional community context is the second contributive referent. Consider your current institutional affiliation. What are the values that bind the members of that institution together? What is the vision of good teaching that provides a sense of common purpose? How is social harmony achieved? Your answers to these questions will help you determine how your constructivist efforts contribute to your institution's sense of community. If no common vision has ever been articulated by members of your institution, you can still reflect on whether or not your efforts are subtly and informally contributing to a sense of community at your institution.

THE CLASSROOM COMMUNITY REFERENT. The third contributive referent is the classroom community context. You will, shortly, be teaching in your own classroom. What type of classroom community will you try to establish? How do you envision you and your future students working together? How will your constructivist efforts contribute to your ability to facilitate a sense of classroom community?

Questioning Discourse

An inquiring student of reflective teaching must be able to question discourse with respect to values of fairness and justice. Constructivist research on learning focuses on how students create knowledge by relating their past experiences and personal purposes to the subjects they are studying. This research examines the *individual* construction of meaning.

We can also inquire into the *social* construction of meaning by studying how knowledge is culturally created. There are two important reasons for being attentive to the cultural creation of knowledge. If we recognize that language is socially constructed, we are in a position to ask about significant past cultural constructions that might guide our present and future actions. By acknowledging that language is a cultural product, we are also in a position to critique the terms we use.

If we are to practice an ethic of caring, we must become comfortable with questioning language. If our language is personally unfair, we can't properly practice the ethic of caring. Language that is stereotypic, narrow, or limiting needs to be questioned. An example will clarify this point.

Suppose you have a student in your class who has been labeled a "troublemaker" by two other teachers, and suppose you are guided by an ethic of caring when working with this student. Would it be helpful to think of this student as a "troublemaker" when trying to confirm his or her best self? How would the word "troublemaker" help you? As Noddings (1984) points out, when you confirm yourself or someone else, you look at things in a positive, growth-oriented way: "Often the cared-for responds in delight and wonder: That is what I mean! That is what I want. The shadowy, always threatening, world of the niggardly and mean falls away" (p. 123).

How could you engage in this uplifting confirmation if you were using such language as "he's a troublemaker"? What does the term "troublemaker" mean, anyway? Aren't great minds often "problems" to small-minded people? As a child, Albert Einstein was "trouble" to some of his teachers. Perhaps the teachers who labelled your student a troublemaker were simply pointing out that the student is disruptive in class. He talks out of turn, he harasses other students, and he is generally a social nuisance. You may find that this behavioral description is fairly accurate, but as an inquiring teacher you must ask what lies behind this student's behavior. Perhaps you can discover a teaching approach that settles him down. The label "troublemaker" was constructed by others. As an inquiring teacher you must question this term or any term that might be personally unfair to your students.

The caring teacher is also careful to use socially just language. Language is a product of our culture. Because we live in a society fraught with overt and subtle social, economic, and political inequalities, our language reflects these inequalities. It becomes tainted by them. Suppose, for example, you are a male middle school math teacher, and you have been raised to think of women as "too emotional" for the exacting logic of mathematics. If you have female students in your class, how could this sexist language possibly help you confirm their best selves? If you take this language seriously, haven't you already decided that, as a math teacher, you can only confirm boys and not girls? If you don't question this language, aren't you likely to be a sexist math teacher selectively caring for your students? Who constructed the language "women are emotional creatures," anyway? Were they infallible beings who can't be questioned? To practice an ethic of caring is to reject social injustice. Each person has a best self—not just the mayor's or millionaire's child. Those who engage in a caring dialogue must be critically alert to the language they use.

A critical perspective on language may at times lead you into uncomfortable situations. As you question the discourse that impacts on your teaching, you may begin to upset some people. They may not understand the importance of critical awareness—even if you tell them that it is necessary for caring teachers. Bernier and Williams (1973) note that educational inquiry "does not require that an individual forsake his beliefs, but merely that he sincerely explore them. . . . This talent may place him in an unpopular role" (p. 404). Though questioning language can be uncomfortable at times, the caring teacher is more interested in confirming individual students than in securing his or her own comfort. The point of caring is to be educationally just. When teachers function this way they not only provide a quality service to their students, they also affirm their own best selves as educating professionals.

Contemplative Practice

The teachers who are the model for this text don't just *say* they are caring and confirming; they practice what they preach. They constantly seek opportunities to cooperatively dialogue with their students. If you are to practice an ethic of caring on yourself, you must do the same. Despite the busy pressures of your modern life-style, you must find time to be self-contemplative. You must seek opportunities to become attuned to your innermost intentions—to examine your best-self purposes for teaching. There are many uniquely meaningful ways to engage in this contemplation. Perhaps you can do this through daily walks or through weekly lunches with a best friend. Whatever approach you take, the important point is to discover a meaningful, contemplative ritual that fits your life-style. In this way you are cultivating your ability to follow an ethic of caring; you are practicing what you preach.

Considering Differing Viewpoints

The ability to consider various viewpoints is also valuable to you as an inquiring student of reflective teaching. Comparing, contrasting, analyzing, and debating the merits and weaknesses of the methods, goals, and philosophies you study helps you recognize your best teaching self.

To facilitate this critical inquiry process, chapters 3 through 6 contain a section entitled *Teacher Insights.* Here you will encounter four fictitious teacher-characters, each of whom personifies a historically significant philosophy of teaching. All of the teacher-characters are inquiring, reflective teachers, but their viewpoints differ on many of the topics and issues covered in this book. As you read what each has to say, you will begin to discover which approaches are most suitable for you.

Because each speaker's viewpoint is partly the result of past experiences and personal purposes, the first *Teacher Insights* section consists of brief autobiographical sketches that will help you understand how and why these teachers came to their respective views. Meet Johnny Jackson, Susan Smith, Dennis Sage and Sylvia Rivera.

TEACHER INSIGHTS

Johnny Jackson, High School English Teacher

I grew up on the south side of Chicago back in the early 1950s. (I'm 46 years old.) My dad was a school custodian, so our family didn't have a lot of money. Still we took advantage of all of the city's cultural resources. It seems like every weekend we went to a museum, a play, a special art exhibit, or whatever. I guess my mom was the main motivator for all of these family outings. She grew up in Alabama and possessed a deep thirst and passion for education. She made sure I worked hard as a student. I can still see her face the day I told her I had been accepted at the University of Chicago.

I majored in English at UC, and I'll never forget one professor who taught a course on James Joyce. Our study of Joyce's novel *Ulysses* was a revelation to me. I couldn't believe so many ideas could be packed into one book. The juxtaposition of the simple everyday lives of the characters with the great ideas of Western civilization was stunning to behold and contemplate—and it still is!

I'm chair of the English Department at a highly respected college preparatory magnet school in the Chicago Public School System. I have my master's degree in English Literature from UC, and I have often thought about going on for my Ph.D. so that I could teach in college. But deep down I realize that my calling is with adolescents. I enjoy turning them on to a vast cultural world they know little about—not because they're not bright enough, but simply because they haven't received the proper exposure. I seem to have my mother's missionary zeal for education—particularly when it comes to the boys. I'm one of the few positive Afro-American role models in their lives. With the help of such creative writers as William Shakespeare and Alice Walker, I can help them discover their potential for a broad and enlightened identity.

Speaking of Shakespeare, I recently read a speech by Dr. Lee Shulman at Stanford University that, for me, captures the essence of the constructivist approach to learning. (By the way, Dr. Shulman is also a graduate of the University of Chicago.) He describes an English teacher who introduces Shakespeare's *Julius Caesar* through an imaginative activity.[2] The teacher asks his students to pretend that they are crew members on the Starship *Enterprise* and are led by the highly respected Captain Kirk. Unfortunately, the captain begins to act strangely, and the crew starts to worry that he will ask them to use the power of the *Enterprise* against the very empire they are sworn to serve. What should the student crew members do? Should they become "revolutionaries" and work to remove Captain Kirk from power, or should they remain "loyalists"? The class discussion raises many feelings. (I know it would for my students because a couple of them have brothers and sisters who are associated with gangs.)

The day after the Starship *Enterprise* discussion the English teacher tells his students that they are going to study a play by Shakespeare that raises many of the same issues they covered yesterday. What an imaginative way to introduce *Julius Caesar!* Shakespeare describes the human comedies and tragedies that are part of our everyday lives, and this teacher found a way to build a meaningful bridge between this great dramatist and his students' past experiences. That's the kind of teaching to which I aspire.

Susan Smith, Elementary School Teacher

My dad is a successful businessman, and I grew up in an affluent suburb outside of Cleveland. I'm 35 years old. I'm quite proud of my dad's accomplishments, and he has always been a big supporter of mine, too. Like when I won the all-school spelling bee as a fifth grader. My strongest opponent was Bobby Watkins, and he never had a chance! I was the power speller supreme, and I got a special kick out of beating a boy.

Both of my parents are well-organized, hardworking people, and thanks to them I know how to use my time well. Sometimes I think I get too task-oriented, but then I realize that life is short and there's much to accomplish. I'm glad I became an elementary school teacher because I can help the next generation acquire the proper work habits.

I like focused people who have goals in life. Sometimes I think I missed my calling and I should have gone into business like my dad. But then I realize that many children today aren't lucky enough to be raised by two hardworking parents. They need someone like me to show them the way. I know this is true because I'll have former students stop by and thank me for that extra push they got in my class.

I'm one of the few women I know who reads the sports pages. My dad used to take me to the Cleveland Browns football games, and I still follow them on television. I like competition; if it's properly managed, it can build character and self-esteem—for girls as well as boys.

I'm currently teaching sixth grade and have a master's degree in Educational Administration and Supervision. My elementary school isn't very big, so our only administrator is the principal. I function as the school's informal assistant principal, for which I get paid extra money. I don't mind the additional responsibilities because I plan to apply for a principalship when there is an opening in my school district. Our school is located in one of the new "professional" suburbs outside of Columbus, Ohio. Most of our children's fathers—and some of the mothers—work for one of the new high-tech firms that are prospering in Columbus. (These vital, dynamic businesses are one of the bright spots in our changing American economy.) Our students are expected to succeed, and they score very high on all of the standardized achievement tests. We are quite proud of this record and have even included an insert in the Sunday paper highlighting the achievement levels of the students in our school district.

I'm also quite proud of my professional accomplishments. I have gone to innumerable "teacher effectiveness" workshops and know how to maximize my students' academic achievements. I can talk for hours about performance objectives, advanced organizers, student engagement rates, lesson transitions, and so on.

One of my heroines is Dr. Madeline Hunter, who is an education professor at the University of California Los Angeles. (In part, I respect all high-achieving women no matter how different their points of view. I applaud both Margaret Thatcher and Geraldine Ferraro.) Dr. Hunter has synthesized educational research into very readable instructional principles and procedures. I highly recommend her book, *Mastery Teaching* (1982). It will help you inquire into the topic of efficient student learning. Teachers are important constructivist mediators for their students. They help them bridge the gap between their unfocused childhood interests and the high-profile, high-performance, problem-solving world of professional life. It is this world that is the future hope for a strong America.

Dennis Sage, Kindergarten Teacher

I sometimes wonder why I'm a teacher. I was raised by an artist mother in the San Francisco Bay area and learned to love the creative process. My mother was a photographer for a local newspaper, but that was just for money. She had to work because my dad left us when I was very young. (I'm 28 years old, and I don't have any brothers or sisters.) Mom built a darkroom in an old dilapidated garage behind our house and did all of her creative work there. She won many prizes and has had her work published in a variety of magazines and books.

I grew up as a member of a loosely affiliated community of artists. I learned how to paint, sculpt, dance, and play the trumpet. I guess that's why I like kindergarten teaching. You can be creative with the children without worrying too much about a bunch of standardized, bureaucratic expectations.

I've studied the works of the great naturalist, John Muir, and I'm an avid backpacker. I believe contemplative inquiry is an important part of quality life, so I have a quiet story time with my students every day. I wonder sometimes what would have happened to our society if our forebears had decided to learn from Native Americans instead of trying to eradicate them. I enjoy studying people and learning about their unique idiosyncrasies. I might have become a novelist, but I didn't want to be a starving artist. (I've seen too many of them in California!)

Instead, I help my students prepare for the wonderful world of literature. They act out all sorts of dramas that we create together. I am fascinated by the Whole Language movement, and I deeply believe that teachers should help their students actively construct their own meanings from what they read. I sometimes think I should get my master's degree in reading and become a reading specialist or teach second grade.

I think I have gone to every creativity workshop there is. I just love learning about new ways to turn kids on to their own creativity. (Have you read *Artistic Intelligences: Implications for Education* (1990), edited by William Moody?) The most important "bridge" in life is between your everyday self and your innermost self—between your profane and sacred sense of life. I want to help my young students learn to balance these two sides of our human nature. I want them to feel special about

themselves and their unique talents and to experience the constant wonder of discovery.

I work for a rural school district in the western foothills of the Sierra Nevada mountains. My children come from all types of families. We've got everything from "hill people" to new professionals in our school district. I guess I enjoy the pluralism in this part of California. It doesn't have the hard edge associated with urban diversity. Californians believe in live and let live. I like that kind of individualism. It can mature into a deep wisdom about life.

One of my favorite educational writers is Max van Manen, who is a professor at the University of Alberta. In 1986 he published a short book entitled *The Tone of Teaching*. In this book he describes authentic teaching as follows:

> A real math teacher is a person who *embodies* math, who *lives* math, who in a strong sense *is* math. . . . A real English teacher tends not only to love reading, writing, and carrying poetry under one arm during coffee break; a real English teacher cannot help but poetize the world—that is, think deeply about human experience through the incantative power of words (pp. 45–46).

I aspire to be this kind of "real teacher." I applaud teachers who have developed a strong educational presence with their students. They understand the aesthetic side of good teaching.

Sylvia Rivera, Middle School Social Studies Teacher

I was born in Puerto Rico in 1961, and my family moved to New York when I was two years old. I have three older brothers and two older sisters. As I was growing up I observed all of their problems adjusting to the United States. My brothers had a hard time finding work. It seems like there was just one barrier after another, and it basically boiled down to one big obstacle: prejudice against people of color. One of my brothers took the easy way out by joining a gang and getting involved in drugs. He's now serving time in Attica, and I visit him once a month. This is very painful to do, and I cry every time I have to say goodbye. He was always so kind and gentle to me when I was young.

I have very loving parents, and they have been quite supportive. They both had low-paying jobs, but they sent all of us to the same Catholic elementary school so that we would get a better education while growing up in the Bronx. This was a big financial burden, but they never complained. We spoke Spanish at home, but the nuns made sure that we spoke only English at school and would never mention our Hispanic background. We were treated as Catholic souls who were accidently born Puerto Ricans.

One nun was special for me. I had her in sixth grade, and she helped me in many ways. She made me feel important, and she taught me to think freely and to question things. As I got older, her ideas got me thinking about all the inequities inflicted upon women. We have fewer opportunities, are paid less, are constantly vulnerable to sexual harassment, and are generally less respected than men. I also have questions about the male domination of the Catholic church and the sexist machismo in the Hispanic community. If I raise these topics with my mother, she just shakes her head and wonders where I get such crazy ideas.

Thanks to an aunt, I managed to get my college degree and teaching certificate from Brooklyn College. She was unable to complete her college education, but she did everything she could to make sure I finished mine. She helped me with money and clothes, and she even let me stay with her one difficult year when I couldn't find a decent job. It took me seven years to get through college, and I couldn't have done it without my aunt. I've read that some educational reformers want college students to wait until they have their undergraduate degrees to learn to teach. Such ideas might be good for the rich, but not for the people I know.

I was certified as an elementary school teacher, but I've always had a keen interest in social studies. I've taken extra graduate courses in history, anthropology, political science and multicultural education. I'm now a social studies specialist at one of the new middle schools in the New York Public School System.

I love turning kids on to social issues—just like that special nun I had in sixth grade. I emphasize multicultural education in my teaching because I want my students to see the important linkages between their distinctive ethnic heritages and the pluralistic society we are trying to become. Instead of celebrating cultural differences, most Americans hide behind sterile, stereotypical middle-class images of good behavior. I know that this is a complex problem compounded by our mass media and our politicians. Have you read *The Ideology of Images in Educational Media* (Ellsworth & Whatley, 1990)? Those in power like our cultural stereotypes; it helps maintain their status and privileges. Where is their Christian sense of justice? Don't they know that Jesus' mission was with the poor?

I want my students to be critical inquirers, not because it is good to be radical, but because it is good to be fair and compassionate. A democratic society should not have so many barriers. Whenever I talk this way to my parents, they get nervous. They say they know their place in society, but do they? Why can't Hispanics share equally in the fruits of our wonderful land?

I'm not sure whether I want to remain in teaching. One part of me believes that through education we can change the power structure in our society. I get inspired when I go to conferences on multicultural education and when I read such texts as *Empowerment through Multicultural Education* (Sleeter, 1990). But the other part of me wonders whether I should get more directly involved in politics and social action. I want to serve as a bridge for a more just world. Can I best do this as a teacher? I have a gift for gab, and I like people. Maybe I should become a lawyer and be a public defender, or even a politician. But I know I would miss my students. Maybe I'll just go on to get my master's degree in multicultural education.

Summary

In this chapter you have learned how to begin to practice good teaching by applying the principles of reflective practice and inquiry to yourself as a student. Though the four teacher-characters have constructed their discourses on teaching out of different life experiences, they share similar professional values with each other and, perhaps, with you. They are caring teachers who want their students to discover their best selves; they believe in the constructivist approach to learning; and they are all committed to processes of educational inquiry—for themselves and for their students. Yet each goes about the process of teaching in a unique way. In the next three chapters you will learn more about each teacher-character's views on several important topics. The autobiographical introductions you have just read will help you understand how and why each teacher-character developed his or her particular views.

As you study chapters 4 through 6, keep in mind an important point. Constructivist learning can't be rushed. Give yourself time to examine each chapter. If you have the opportunity, discuss your inquiries with your student peers and with an experienced teacher. If it's helpful, think of the next three chapters as a journey of discovery. (Is this a useful metaphor?) Maintain an open, exploratory approach as you study each chapter, and try to be as personally honest in your inquiries as you possibly can. Remember the overall purpose for studying the chapters: you are clarifying and confirming your *best teaching self*.

Personal-Professional Inquiry

The focus of this chapter is on preparing you to practice constructivist learning on yourself in your role as a student who is learning to teach. Five categories of questions can be distilled from this chapter's discussion of reflective practice and inquiry. You can use these questions as a guide for examining the teacher-characters' biographical statements. You will use these same five categories of questions in chapters 4 through 6 to examine the topics of problem-solving, curriculum leadership, and classroom community leadership.

1. *Remembered Anecdotes:* Can you remember any teachers who were like one of the teacher-characters? What do you remember about them? Do you remember them positively or negatively?
2. *Role Models:* Have you experienced a parent, relative, teacher, or some other significant adult who was a positive role model as a teacher? Were their perspectives on education similar to any of the four teacher-characters' views? Could one or more of the teacher-characters serve as a positive role model for the type of teacher you want to become?
3. *Personal Metaphors:* Using the term "good teacher" as your nucleus, create a cluster. Examine the personal metaphors in your cluster. Are any of them similar to metaphors used in the teacher-characters' autobiographical statements?
4. *Community Referents:* Do you think the four teacher-characters would be good members of a teaching community? Would they all contribute equally to the vitality of a school? Would you like to have one or more of them in your school community? Why or why not?
5. *Teacher-Characters' Discourse:* Do you think all four of the teacher-characters would be fair and just teachers? Did you find yourself questioning any of the perspectives in each teacher-character's autobiographical statement?

Endnotes

1. Rico, G. L. (1983). *Writing the natural way: Using right-brain techniques to release your expressive powers.* Los Angeles: J. P. Tarcher. See in particular pp. 36–37.
2. Shulman, L. S. (1989, January), *Aristotle had it right: On knowledge and pedagogy.* Keynote address at the meeting of The Holmes Group. (Available from The Holmes Group, 501 Erickson Hall, East Lansing, MI 48824–1034)

References

ABBS, P. (1984). Education and the living image: Reflections on imagery, fantasy, and the art of recognition. In D. Sloan (Ed.), *Toward the recovery of wholeness: Knowledge, education, and human values* (pp. 103–124). New York: Teachers College Press.

BERNIER, N. R., & WILLIAMS, J. E. (1973). *Beyond beliefs: Ideological foundations of American education.* Englewood Cliffs, NJ: Prentice-Hall.

CASSIRER, E. (1946). *Language and myth* (S. Langer, Trans.). New York: Dover. (Original work published 1925)

CONNELLY, F. M., & CLANDININ, D. J. (1985). Personal practical knowledge and the modes of knowing: Relevance for teaching and learning. In E. W. Eisner (Ed.), *Learning and teaching the ways of knowing,* (84th Yearbook of the National Society for the Study of Education, Part II) (pp. 174–198). Chicago: University of Chicago Press.

EISNER, E. W. (1985). *The educational imagination: On the design and evaluation of school programs* (2nd ed.). New York: Macmillan.

ELBAZ, F. (1981). The teacher's "practical knowledge": Report of a case study. *Curriculum Inquiry, 11,* 43–71.

ELLSWORTH, E., & WHATLEY, M. (Eds.). (1990). *The ideology of images in educational media.* New York: Teachers College Press.

GREENE, M. (1988). *The dialectic of freedom.* New York: Teachers College Press.

HUNTER, M. (1982). *Mastery teaching.* El Secundo, CA: TIP Publications.

MOODY, W. (Ed.) (1990). *Artistic intelligences: Implications for education.* New York: Teachers College Press.

NODDINGS, N. (1984). *Caring: A feminine approach to ethics and moral education.* Berkeley: University of California Press.

RICO, G. L. (1983). *Writing the natural way: Using right-brain techniques to release your expressive powers.* Los Angeles: J. P. Tarcher.

SLEETER, C. (Ed.). (1990). *Empowerment through multicultural education.* Albany, NY: State University of New York Press.

VAN MANEN, M. (1986). *The tone of teaching.* Richmond Hill, Ontario: Scholastic-TAB.

CHAPTER 4

Inquiring into Educational Problem Solving

Introduction

In chapter 1 you learned that good teachers make up to 200 decisions every day. Most of these decisions are fairly routine and don't require much time or energy, but "smooth sailing" days are rare in the actual classroom. Teachers must be prepared to confront challenging problems. In this chapter you will inquire into the topic of educational problem solving.

Educational problem solving is different from technical and administrative problem solving. The referent for technical problem solving is a particular protocol, such as a standardized procedure for diagnosing student problems. The referent for administrative problem solving is district and building policy. Management has decided what students will learn, how they will be disciplined, etc. Teachers have the "problem" of implementing this policy.

The referent for educational problem solving is far more complex. It includes the ethic of caring and the constructivist approach to teaching. The most important outcome of educational problem solving is the students' meaningful learning. To practice inquiring, reflective teaching you need to become a good educational problem solver. This chapter is designed to help you learn about this topic.

To help you construct your own professional knowledge, the chapter begins with a general description of educational problem solving. Then the four teacher-characters will offer their views on how to be an educational problem solver. In the Personal-Professional Inquiry section at the end of the chapter, you will reflect on what educational problem solving means to you.

General Characteristics of Educational Problem Solving

Good teachers think not only about what, how, and why they teach, they also carefully consider the educational problems they encounter. Most of this reflection occurs before and after instruction because there simply isn't enough time for careful deliberation during class. Just as other aspects of their classroom work differ, educational problem-solving techniques vary from teacher to teacher. However, most teachers roughly follow a four-step process:

1. Reflecting on the learning situation.
2. Identifying the problem.
3. Trying out one or more solutions.
4. Engaging in further inquiry.

Reflecting on the Learning Situation

Learning situations in teaching include all the immediacies of the classroom moment—something so complex that it can't fully be described. Each teacher has individual beliefs, personal metaphors, values, feelings, intuitions, habits, routines, and goals. Each teacher must interact with approximately 30 students who also have their own beliefs, personal metaphors, values, feelings, intuitions, habits, routines, and goals. In addition, parents, the principal, other school staff, and members of the community expect teachers to consider their beliefs, values, and goals as well. The complexity of any moment in the action-present of teaching is diagrammed in Figure 4–1.

Learning situations are so complex that no single method of problem solving can be applied in all cases. As a result, numerous differing—and often competing—interpretations of educational problem solving exist today. When you face a learning problem you must reflect on the situation to identify the factors that seem most important in that particular case. Then you will be better able to choose the method that seems most appropriate.

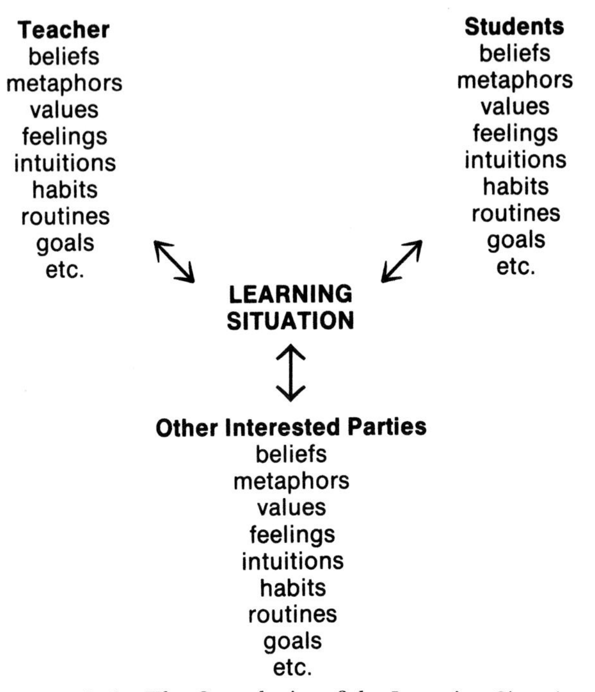

FIGURE 4–1 The Complexity of the Learning Situation.

Identifying the Problem

Fortunately teachers don't have to understand all the complexities of a specific classroom situation to begin to identify problems that must be solved. Different teachers may, of course, define a specific problem in very different ways. For example, one teacher may see a student's reading difficulty as a phonetic problem, while another teacher may regard it as a motivation problem. *Both* teachers might be "right"! Or, they both might be "wrong" because their definitions of the problem do not lead to solutions. Their problem solving may be unproductive because their teaching habits and routines prevent them from undertaking the necessary diagnostic work. One teacher might be "right," and one teacher might be "wrong." And there would be reasons for this, too. (Perhaps you can think of some.) Whatever the case, the point is that, because of the complexities of the learning situation, teachers may define a learning problem in different ways.

We can further refine this discussion by distinguishing between bounded and unbounded problems (Weizenbaum, 1981). A *bounded problem* is relatively clear and its solution is readily apparent to teachers with different beliefs and habits. For example, a student has an addition problem in math because he doesn't understand the distinction between the number columns. The definition of this problem would be apparent to most informed teachers, and a good problem-solving teacher with a background in math and math methods could develop a strategy for solving it successfully.

Consider another example of a bounded problem. A high school social studies teacher has a class of students who are confused about the chronology of major events in United States history. Drawing on her academic and methods background, she deliberates over various solutions to this problem. Perhaps she decides to require students to memorize a very explicit time line. Perhaps she decides on another strategy. (Can you think of another possible solution?) Whatever she decides to do, the problem is fairly straightforward, or bounded.

An *unbounded problem* is far more complex because it can legitimately be defined in many different ways. Or, information about the problem may be incomplete, and the solution for solving the problem may not be readily apparent or may not yet exist. Two examples will illustrate these characteristics of unbounded problems.

A white elementary school teacher ponders why one of her black students is hostile to her and to the other students, many of whom are also black. How can the teacher define this problem? Is it a psychological problem? If so, which psychological theory provides the best insight? Should she turn to the school psychologist for help? Perhaps the problem is sociological. Is it a personal problem of adjustment, a problem of family breakdown, a problem related to race relations, or . . . ? What information should the teacher collect to help define and solve the problem? Perhaps there's more than one good solution.

Consider another unbounded problem. A high school teacher encounters rowdy students in the study hall he supervises and has a very difficult time settling them down. How shall he define this problem? Is it a problem of school organization? Perhaps there shouldn't be any study halls because the students rarely do their homework at school anyway. Is this a historical problem—a change in the study habits of today's adolescents? Are the students learning proper values at home? Do they find school boring? Are they motivated to complete schoolwork only when they are studying in a structured, closely supervised setting? If so, what causes their lack of motivation? Perhaps only some of the students are rowdy, but their behavior sets the tone in the study hall. Could these students be identified and removed? Where to? If there is a solution, it must respond to the complexities of the problem. Unlike bounded problems, which generally have easy solutions, unbounded problems are tough to resolve. A combination of several solutions may be necessary, or, again, there may be no ready solution.

Trying Out Solutions

Consider again the elementary school teacher with the hostile student. Perhaps she will first try two solutions that she formulated with the help of the school psychologist. In a quiet, one-on-one setting she invites the student to talk about his feelings. She also gives the student a highly desirable duty that lets him know that he is a valued member of the class. For example, she could ask the student to take the lunch money to the office.

Engaging in Further Inquiry

If the first problem-solving strategies don't work, teachers must engage in further inquiry. Gathering more information, talking to different people, or examining one's own feelings and intuitions may lead to new insights about the problem. Unbounded problems are more likely to require further inquiry than bounded problems.

The elementary school teacher must continue to probe her student's perceptions, to deliberate, to collaborate, to examine her own teaching limitations until . . . until . . . until she finds a resolution to the difficulty. She is committed to this extensive problem solving because she cares. As a student of constructivist learning theory she knows that she must not take the student's hostile attitude personally. Though this hostility is dysfunctional, it is an understandable personal construction based partly on the student's past experiences. It will not be overcome easily; perhaps it can not be overcome at all. The teacher knows that she must be patient and that, for the sake of this student's future, she must not give up. As Noddings (1984) observed, the caring teacher "receives not just the 'response' but the student. What he says matters, whether it is right or wrong, and she probes gently for clarification, interpretation, contribution" (p. 176).

The inquiring problem solver is willing to tackle unbounded as well as bounded problems—even though the unbounded problems may necessitate further inquiry or may be predicaments that are never fully resolved. The non-inquiring problem solver, on the other hand, deals only with routine classroom decisions that don't require much time or energy. Ignoring the complexities of learning situations, such a teacher defines all problems simplistically. The teacher has no sense that the problem might be defined differently and makes no attempt to experimentally try out a solution or solutions. After all, if one is right, what's the point of experimenting? Finally, this non-inquiring teacher rejects the idea of further inquiry. The problem has been solved—end of discussion. Do you know anyone who approaches problems in such an uninquiring way?

John Dewey described the complex thinking process involved in inquiring educational problem solving in his book *How We Think* (1933). Grimmett (1988) summarized Dewey's analysis of problem solving as follows. First we reflect on a problem when we experience "a state of doubt, hesitation, perplexity, or mental difficulty" (Grimmett, p. 6). Next we seek to transform this problematic experience "into a situation that is clear, coherent, settled, harmonious" (Dewey, pp. 100–101). We arrive at a tentative conclusion that is partly based on our past experiences with solving problems. This tentative conclusion is, in part, an inference that what we did in the past to solve our problems will work again. We act tentatively because we do not know if our inference will lead to a productive solution. Sometimes our problem-solving inferences are correct (particularly with bounded problems), and sometimes they are not. Because we act tentatively we are willing to engage in further inquiry until we arrive at a conclusion that we feel is "trustworthy" (Dewey, p. 47). This means that we must be "willing to endure suspense and to undergo the trouble of searching" (Dewey, p. 16). This suspense is based on a "paradox" of problem solving (Grimmett, p. 8). We cannot know whether our tentative efforts will be successful until we act, but it is difficult to act without knowing exactly what to do. To be active problem solvers, we must persist despite this paradox.

TEACHER INSIGHTS

Johnny Jackson

Students' academic problems should be your highest priority as a teacher. My strategy for dealing with them is generally known as *academic problem solving* because it has a humanistic or academic emphasis on classical content.

I subscribe to the constructivist theory of learning. I believe that students "construct their own meaning of new information and ideas on the basis of their existing knowledge; learning is not a matter of passively taking up 'static' information" (MacKinnon & Erickson, 1988, p. 121). Teachers must be bridge-makers. They must actively create bridges between the formal knowledge of a subject and the past experiences and personal purposes of their students.

Donald Schon (1988), a leading researcher on reflective practice, has described a four-step process of academic problem solving. Here is an adaptation of his recommendations.

1. Observe carefully what your student says and does. Understand the learning problem from his or her point of view.
2. Think of what your student says and does as a puzzle you want to solve. You must assume that somehow the student is making sense. Unfortunately this type of "making sense" may be unrelated to the requirements of the subject matter in your lesson.
3. Invent bridges between your student's understanding and the subject matter.
4. You have successfully solved the puzzle when your instructional bridges are meaningful to the student. When this occurs, a connection has been made between the student's naive knowledge and the privileged knowledge of the subject matter.

To serve as a bridge builder, of course, you must understand the academic side of the river: You must have a thorough command of your subject matter. You must also have acquired a good, empathetic understanding of your students' pertinent past experiences and personal purposes. This is the other side of the river.

You can try your hand at academic problem solving now, even without your own class. You'll need the help of your peers and a good coach—someone who is a strong academic problem solver and a patient guide.

First let's look at how a good coach helps Jill, a social studies student teacher, practice academic problem solving. Jill has just taught her students a lesson on the relationship between propaganda and social prejudice. One student, John, was upset by the lesson. Jill's supervisor, Ms. Lincoln, helps her reflect on this problem.

Jill: I think most of the students were fascinated by the dramatic changes in the public images of the "good" mother and wife that occurred after World War II. During the war, patriotic women went to work each day to help their sons and husbands defeat the enemy. Once the war was over, women were supposed to return to the home to provide a steady, loving presence—like Beaver's mother in "Leave It To Beaver." If a woman worked she was seen as the cause of all sorts of social problems, like juvenile delinquency and divorce. I wanted the students to examine why the images of the good mother and wife had changed so quickly in 1945. Was it mainly due to men's fear that women would compete with them for scarce factory jobs? Questions like that. During the lesson, I could tell that John was getting more and more upset.

Ms. Lincoln: What was upsetting him?

Jill: I wasn't sure, so I asked John if he had any reactions to the lesson. He was kind of sullen, but he did softly mutter that mothers should be at home. I didn't know what to do. I was teaching an inquiry lesson, and he was taking it so personally!

Ms. Lincoln: Did you try to have a private conversation with John after the lesson?

Jill: I thought about it, but he seemed too upset to want to talk to me.

Ms. Lincoln: Perhaps he was, but you could have extended an invitation for a private talk anyway, and then let him accept or decline the invitation. In fact, you can still make the offer. To return to the lesson, is there anything else you might have done with John's comment?

Jill: I don't know. Nothing came to mind at the time.

Ms. Lincoln: It's hard to think on your feet, but what about now? How could you get a student to explore such stereotypic phrases as "a woman's place is in the home"?

Jill: I suppose I could ask the student why he feels that way.

Ms. Lincoln: He's not the only one who feels this way.

Jill: I could get into their feelings—why people feel that women should stay at home.

Ms. Lincoln: You might want to try another approach. Once one student shares a personal image, ask the class to contribute their images of women. Get them inquiring into the metaphors they use. Instead of just focusing on one student's image, and the feelings surrounding that image, open up the dialogue. If a student gets fixated on an image, don't get fixated on him or her. Remember, you're trying to conduct an inquiry lesson. What do you think?

Jill: Maybe I was overly anxious for students to see the sexism in the changing images of women at the end of the war. Maybe I don't need to push so hard. Perhaps I can figure out some different ways students can explore the personal images they carry about women.

Ms. Lincoln: You might also want to consider ways to switch to a related topic when feelings get ruffled. What about our changing images of the Japanese and the Germans during and after World War II? Couldn't that topic also help you with your objective, which was to explore the relationship between propaganda and social prejudice?

Jill: I see your point. I'll give that some thought.

This dialog was inspired by an article by Erickson and MacKinnon (1988). You might want to refer to the article for more examples of coaching dialogues. Once you're familiar with the concept, I recommend that you design situations in which you can receive coaching assistance. In a university classroom you can set up role-playing scenarios where you teach "students" with specific academic learning problems. One or more coaches, either faculty members or other students, can serve as coaches to help you define and solve the problems. After you've had sufficient role-playing experience you can move into an actual classroom to practice academic problem solving with the assistance of a knowledgeable and supportive coach.

Whether you are role-playing or solving actual classroom learning problems, keep an inquiring attitude. Stay open to the complexities of the learning situation and to the way you have framed the problem. Maintain an experimental posture toward your solution and be ready to inquire further into the problem. Remember, academic problem solving is a critical part of good teaching. If you can't build meaningful bridges between your students' naive knowledge and the subject matter you are teaching, they're stuck on their side of the river. Please give them the opportunity to cross those bridges.

Susan Smith

When you solve a learning problem, you construct judgments as to what the problem is and how it should be solved. I recommend that you continually review the quality of your judgment with the help of research on students' learning achievements. This is not a difficult way to solve problems, but you can't do it if you don't know this research.

Think of your problem solving as a practical judgment that is based on either an empirically flawed or an empirically sound argument (Fenstermacher, 1987). An empirically sound argument is one that can be supported by evidence gathered through careful formal or informal research. For example, "If students attend class regularly and study effectively, then they will get good grades." An empirically flawed argument has one or more if-then premises that can't be supported by research. For example, "If a student fails the final exam, then he will still get an 'A' in the course."

Good educational problem solving is based on using empirically sound arguments. Consider an example adapted from an article by Fenstermacher (1986). Suppose a teacher is confronted with too many distracting discipline problems. Students are not achieving as efficiently as he would like, and their test scores are lower than they should be. The teacher makes this initial judgment: If he structures his lessons better, then he will have fewer discipline problems and his students' test scores will go up.

But then he begins to wonder whether his empirical judgment is sound. He recalls that educational research on a method known as direct instruction indicates that this teaching strategy helps minimize discipline problems. He knows that direct instruction is a highly focused type of teaching that requires students to be on task at all times. He also knows that there are numerous specific prescriptions associated with direct instruction. The teacher decides to review the research on this method and finds prescriptions such as this one:

> Students should know what work they are accountable for, how to get help when they need it, and what to do when they finish. Performance should be monitored for completion and accuracy, and students should receive timely and specific feedback. (Brophy & Good, 1986, p. 364)

He adapts these prescriptions to fit his situation and implements the direct teaching solution he has devised.

Next he carefully studies the consequences of his action. Are the distracting discipline problems occurring less frequently? Is student achievement improving? Are some students rebelling against the added structure in the classroom day? (He recalls educational research that indicates that teachers who are too direct in their instruction inhibit student motivation.) As new evidence comes in he willingly reconsiders his decision to implement direct instruction by identifying and reviewing his empirical judgments.

Here are the problem-solving steps that this exemplary teacher followed, and that I hope you will follow:

1. Identify the learning achievement problem that you must solve.
2. Consider ways to solve this problem.
3. Identify the empirical judgment(s) associated with step #2. (Remember, these are if-then premises associated with students' learning achievements.)
4. Determine how educational research supports, challenges, or modifies your empirical judgment(s).
5. Make final adjustments in your problem solving in light of step #4.
6. Act to solve the problem.
7. Study the consequences of your actions and, in accordance with the dictates of educational research, make any further adjustments in your problem-solving behavior.
8. Continue this cycle until you have resolved the problem in an empirically sound manner.

You can practice the discipline of constructing your own empirically sound arguments. In a university classroom you can set up a role-playing situation in which a problem emerges. First you identify the problem and consider how to solve it. With the help of your instructor and your peers, identify the empirical argument or arguments in your proposed solution and consider ways to verify and strengthen, modify, or refute these if-then premises. Apply your refined solution to the practical judgments in role-playing settings, you can move to an actual classroom to further practice this disciplined form of problem solving.

I agree with Johnny Jackson that you should maintain an inquiring classroom to further practice this disciplined form of problem solving.

I agree with Johnny Jackson that you should maintain an inquiring attitude throughout your problem-solving deliberations. You can never be certain that you have correctly diagnosed an achievement problem, so be prepared to think of different ways of framing and then solving the problem. Remember, you want your students to be winners in our society. If they are successful, our society is the actual winner because their achievements contribute to our overall social and economic stability.

Dennis Sage

To me, so-called problem solving is really an intuitive matter between you and your students. Phrases such as "deliberating over learning problems" are too academic and formal for my taste. It's too cold. Good teachers develop rapport with their students. They find a way to mesh their personalities with their students'. Once teachers are attuned to their students, a lot of so-called problems disappear.

Teaching is about motivation. When you've got motivated students, the classroom is alive with energy. You've got to be enthusiastic about your subject matter, and you've got to want to work with your students. If they sense that you don't want to be with them, all the deliberation in the world isn't going to help you solve your teaching problems.

Teaching is a passionate love affair, and it is this passion that engages your intuitive abilities. Certainly you will encounter problems as a teacher, but just listen carefully to yourself and to your students and appropriate solutions will begin to emerge. Studying educational research distracts you from your intuitive listening. How much of this research was conducted in passionate settings, anyway? What wisdom is discovered through carefully controlled empirical research? To be responsive, you must be connected to the teaching present—to the teaching moment. One of my favorite books is Leonard's *Education and*

Ecstasy (1968). Here's how he describes the high moments in teaching, which for me are the final solution to educational problems.

> How many of those times do you remember? *Something happens.* A delicate warmth slides into parts of your being you didn't even realize were cold. The marrow of your bones begins to thaw. You feel a little lurch as your own consciousness, the teacher's voice, the entire web of sound and silence that holds the class together, the room itself, the very flow of time all shift to a different level. . . . How many teachable days? One out of a hundred? Then you are of the favored. (pp. 8-9)

Let me ask you three questions. Do you really solve the problems in your life using an academic problem-solving or an empirically based judgment perspective? If you became more academically or empirically versed, would you be better able to solve your problems? Where is the wisdom in such formal, analytical approaches?

If these questions got you thinking, you might want to keep looking for the problem-solving style that fits you as a person. If you can't be your own person in the classroom, how in the world are you going to connect with your students? If you're not authentic, how are you going to establish rapport? And without rapport, how can you be intuitive?

I believe in *intuitive problem solving*. Open up, enjoy working with your students, and allow your intuition to come into play. Teaching is like dancing with a partner. Get into the rhythms! You can't solve all the problems of the world, but you can share the joy of learning with your students. Here are some specific recommendations on how to do this.

1. Get to know your students as unique individuals. Look for opportunities to talk to them about their past experiences, current interests, and future goals. As much as you can, get to know their family and community backgrounds. All of this information will help you contemplate the best course of action for each of your students.
2. Maintain a good, poised mood when you are at school. If you are unhappy, if you feel too much stress, your students will know it. You won't be helping them feel good about their education, and you will be limiting your intuitive capacities. An unbalanced personal-professional life-style may be your greatest obstacle to becoming a sensitive, inquiring teacher.
3. Allow yourself to feel your students' learning anxieties. If you were in their shoes, what would you be feeling? To be an intuitive problem solver you must be empathetic and imaginative.

4. Think about the learning problem and its solution from the best-self perspective of each of your students. Your problem-solving referent should be each student's personal aspirations, not some academic or research tradition. How can they have a happier, more fulfilled life? What is best for them in the long run?
5. Whatever solution you try out, maintain a thoughtful composure. Teaching and learning aren't easy because life isn't easy. The art of living is based on contemplative self-discipline, and you model this art for your students by solving their learning problems in a composed and wise way. As your students get older, they will discover their own ways to practice a contemplative discipline, and they will thank you for demonstrating this possibility to them. We can never be free from life's problems, but we can all find our paths to personal wisdom.

These recommendations are based on Goldberg's (1983) ideas. If they sound good to you, you may want to work at strengthening your intuitive abilities. This is a highly personal and passionate matter, but it never hurts to get more information on the topic. There are many good books on intuition.

In his book *The Intuitive Edge: Understanding Intuition and Applying It in Everyday Life* (1983), Goldberg recommends that you keep an intuition journal. This is a journal in which you record your spontaneous and innermost thoughts, feelings, and sensations. Goldberg describes intuitions as the "sparks" of our minds (p. 20). They ignite our deliberate, rational plans, our judgments about others, and our careful analyses. Our intuitions provide us with personal intimations that we can then turn into more objective information through careful educational problem solving.

An intuition journal can help you remember and work with your own personal intuitive sparks on teaching and learning matters. When you get a spontaneous thought, feeling, or sensation, write it down as soon as possible. If you have the time, describe the circumstances of your intuitive flash. Did it come to you while you were taking a shower? Was there something you were thinking about? Did you get a clear insight or just a hazy feeling? Then, when you have more reflective time, go back to your initial journal entries and give them some more thought. What do you think of your intuition now? Is it a useful idea? Does it help you get better insight into one of your problems? Can you use your intuition in your educational problem solving? Make notes of your reflections in your journal. This way you will have your authentic thoughts and feelings concerning your intuitions as well as the sparks themselves. By keeping this two-part journal you will sharpen your ability to draw on your intuitions to help you in your problem solving.

The problem solving technique I am describing is not mechanical at all. You must first be very committed to your students; then your intuitions about their best selves will begin to emerge. You are not trying to help them *get ahead* in their lives, but rather to *get into* their lives. This metaphorical distinction is critical to understanding the advice I am offering. I hope you will give it some thought.

Sylvia Rivera

Classrooms are part of a society and they reflect its particular history. The problems that teachers face in the classroom occur within a broader social-historical context. Therefore I recommend *historically aware problem solving.* Earlier you were introduced to the distinction between bounded and unbounded problems. Bounded problems are like a 10-piece puzzle. Anyone with a little skill and some common sense can put it together. Unbounded problems are like a 500-piece puzzle. It takes time, effort, patience, and insight to put all the pieces in the right place.

Modern society is full of 500-piece puzzles, and sometimes the pieces get mixed up. Sometimes I need to look beyond the school, in the society at large, to find the pieces I need to complete my classroom puzzles. Society's problems influence what happens in our classrooms.

Let me illustrate this broad social perspective on teaching problems with an example. When I experience a discipline problem in class, I look for historical insight to define both the problem and its solution. Suppose I have a student who acts out in class. I ask myself, "Where did this behavior start?" Usually my answer is, "in the home environment." Then I analyze the student's home environment to determine what might be encouraging the acting-out behavior. Perhaps the student comes from a single-parent family led by a hardworking, highly stressed mother. What social forces are operating on this type of family? What caused the student's mother and father to separate? Why isn't there a better supportive network in our society to help single parents raise their children? Is the mother working in a job where she is underpaid and overstressed? How many women in our society get tracked into that kind of work? Why is it that men generally can find more interesting and higher-paid work?

I could go on and on with such questions, but I'm sure you get the point. Teaching problems generally are not isolated from specific social problems, and these social problems have a history. Teaching takes place in a complex historical ecology of interconnected social forces. Only the naive, unaware teacher would deny this dimension to educational difficulties. I like what Beyer and Apple (1988) say about the unbounded nature of educational problems:

> We need to think about education *relationally*. We need to see it as being integrally connected to the cultural, political, and economic institutions of the larger society, institutions that may be strikingly unequal by race, gender, and class. (p. 4)

Think about what Beyer and Apple are saying. If, for example, racism occurs in the private, commercial, and political sectors of your community, it will inevitably have an impact upon the teaching problems you face. Problems *in* the classroom are closely tied to problems *outside* the classroom. It's that simple and that complex.

I recommend that you persistently examine the social context of the problems you face. Look at a classroom difficulty as *historically unbounded*. See its relationship to the broad cultural, political, and economic forces of our time. Once you have framed the problem in this historical way, decide upon an appropriate solution. Usually when you define a problem as broadly as I do, you discover you can't solve the problem by yourself. You will need help. Historically conceived problems generally require collaborative action.

Let's return to the acting-out problem. If there is a historical context to the problem, other teachers should also be experiencing the same or similar problems. Broad social problems generally don't impact on just some classrooms. If I find that other teachers are experiencing similar difficulties in their classes, I encourage my peers to work with me to solve the problem together. This professional collaboration might extend to other service professionals in the building (the school psychologist, the school nurse, the school administrators), to other service professionals in the community (social workers, health care providers, police), and to other responsible members of the community (parents, community activists, local politicians).

My problem-solving approach has led me to recognize that a highly participative school organization is a necessary requirement for historically aware problem solving. In chapter 9 you will read more about this type of school organization.

To summarize, I recommend that you deliberate on problems as follows:

1. Identify a classroom learning problem.
2. Analyze the historical context of the problem. How is this problem

related to the cultural, political, and economic conditions of our society?

3. Seek ways to collaborate with others to solve the problem. Recognize that this type of collaboration may require the establishment of a participative school operation. The way your school is organized may be part of the problem. Can you do anything about this?
4. Implement your solution, but keep a critical eye on the consequences of your actions. Were you just treating a symptom, or did you really find a cure for the illness?

Persistent historically aware problem solving leads toward a particular educational orientation known as *transformative teaching.* As you become sensitive to the historical context of problems, you increasingly recognize the need to transform our society. Despite what you might hear from historically unaware, image-conscious politicians and popular media, our modern society is no utopia. Inequities pervade all aspects of our lives. With the help of transformative teaching, students can gain insight into these inequities and, I hope, discover their own collaborative role in the historic challenges of creating a better society. One of the committed transformative teachers of our generation wrote: "Teaching in this [historically aware] mode is a Utopian challenge to social limits on thought and feeling. I can't imagine a more optimistic way to go about education" (Shor, 1987, pp. 269–270).

I hope that you will be an optimistic educational problem solver in this socially transformative spirit. Teachers can make a difference; in their own small ways, they can help alleviate the social, economic, and political inequities in our society. I hope that you will ponder the link between your specific teaching problems and the historic challenges of our times.

Personal-Professional Inquiry

In chapter 3 you studied five categories of constructivist learning questions: remembered anecdotes, role models, personal metaphors, community referents, and teacher-characters' discourse. Now you will explore these questions with reference to the topic of educational problem solving.

1. Describe your past experiences with problem solving. What was positive about these experiences? What was negative about them?
2. Make a list of people who served as your role models for problem solving. The list may include a parent, relative, teacher, or other significant adults. Describe how and why each person was a positive or negative role model.
3. Using the term "educational problem solving" as your nucleus, create a cluster. Select one or more personal metaphors from your cluster and compose a paragraph that explores what each metaphor means to you.
4. Think about the various communities to which you belong. How would you contribute to these communities as a confident educational problem solver? For example, you may be studying this text as part of a classroom community. As you work on your personal problem-solving standards, how might your efforts contribute to the quality of interactions in your class? When you become a member of a school faculty in the future, how might your problem-solving efforts contribute to the professionalism in the building?
5. What do you think about the four teacher-characters' advice? Would you want to have any of these individuals as your cooperating teacher during student teaching, or would you want a cooperating teacher who had developed an eclectic mix of the problem-solving approaches covered in this chapter?
6. What other questions occur to you as you inquire into the topic of educational problem solving?

Further Readings

The following list of books recommended by Nickerson (1988) will help you learn more about the topic of educational problem solving.

Adams, J. L. (1974). *Conceptual blockbusting: A guide to better ideas.* San Francisco: Freeman.

Bransford, J. D., & Stein, B. S. (1984). *The IDEAL problem solver: A guide for improving thinking, learning, and creativity.* New York: Freeman.

Halpern, D. F. (1984). *Thought and knowledge: An introduction to critical thinking.* Hillsdale, NJ: Erlbaum.

Hayes, J. R. (1981). *The complete problem solver.* Philadelphia: The Franklin Institute Press.

Ruggiero, V. R. (1984). *The art of thinking: A guide to critical and creative thought.* New York: Harper & Row.

References

BEYER, L. E., & APPLE, M. W. (1988). Values and politics in the curriculum. In L. E. Beyer & M. W. Apple (Eds.), *The curriculum: Problems, politics, and possibilities* (pp. 3–16). Albany, NY: State University of New York Press.

BROPHY, J. E., & GOOD, T. L. (1986). Teacher behavior and student achievement. In M. C. Wittrock (Ed.), *Handbook of research on teaching* (3rd ed.) (pp. 328–375). New York: Macmillan.

DEWEY, J. (1933). *How we think: A restatement of the relation of reflective thinking to the educative process.* Chicago: D. C. Heath.

ERICKSON, G. L. & MACKINNON, A. M. (1988). Taking Schon's ideas to a science teaching practicum. In P. P. Grimmett & G. L. Erickson (Eds.), *Reflection in teacher education* (pp. 113–137). New York: Teachers College Press.

FENSTERMACHER, G. D. (1986). Philosophy of research on teaching: Three aspects. In M. C. Wittrock (Ed.), *Handbook of research on teaching* (3rd ed.) (pp. 37–49). New York: Macmillan.

FENSTERMACHER, G. D. (1987). A reply to my critics. *Educational Theory, 37,* 413–421

GOLDBERG, P. (1983). *The intuitive edge: Understanding intuition and applying it in everyday life.* Los Angeles: J. P. Tarcher.

GRIMMETT, P. P. (1988). The nature of reflection and Schon's conception in perspective. In P. P. Grimmett & G. L. Erickson (Eds.), *Reflection in teacher education* (pp. 5–15). New York: Teachers College Press.

LEONARD, G. B. (1968). *Education and ecstasy.* New York: Dell.

NICKERSON, R. S. (1988). On improving thinking through instruction. In E. Z. Rothkopf (Ed.), *Review of Research in Education, 15,* 3–57. Washington, DC: American Educational Research Association.

NODDINGS, N. (1984). *Caring: A feminine approach to ethics and moral education.* Berkeley: University of California Press.

SCHON, D. (1988). Coaching reflective teaching. In P. P. Grimmett & G. L. Erickson (Eds.), *Reflection in teacher education* (pp. 21–22). New York: Teachers College Press.

SHOR, I. (1987). *Critical teaching and everyday life* (2nd ed.). Chicago: University of Chicago Press.

WEIZENBAUM, J. (1984). Limits in the use of computer technology: Need for a man-centered science. In D. Sloan (Ed.), *Toward the recovery of wholeness: Knowledge, education, and human values* (pp. 149–158) New York: Teachers College Press.

CHAPTER 5

Inquiring into Curriculum Leadership

Introduction

This chapter invites investigation of the inquiring, reflective teacher's role as a leader in curriculum development. The discussion begins with a realistic look at whether teachers need to concern themselves with curriculum at all, and what the consequences may be if they choose not to do so. Curriculum issues include such questions as what teachers should teach, how they should teach it, and how they should evaluate their students' learning. Like most of the other topics covered in this text, the issue of curriculum leadership draws different responses from different people. Therefore the third section of the chapter is devoted to the four teacher-characters' views on curriculum leadership. The Personal-Professional Inquiry section will guide you in formulating your own opinion on curriculum leadership.

Leading or Following: The Choice Is Yours

To a beginning teacher, curriculum is one area of professional responsibility that seems relatively unproblematic. Given all of the other concerns one must face as a teacher, it is tempting to leave decisions about what to teach entirely to others. Why worry about choice of content when school districts or state departments of education supply lists of objectives and skills, pre-formulated courses of study, or curriculum guides? Or perhaps the curriculum consists of the items on a standardized test on which students are expected to excel. At the very least teachers can surely rely on an approved textbook by renowned subject matter experts who selected and organized important content matter in the best manner—can't they?

The authors of this book recognize the great demands placed upon teachers that lead them to seek ways to simplify their lives. Routine, mechanical decision making may seem unavoidable in a work environment as harried, demanding, and sometimes threatening as that of most public schools. Teachers may choose to limit the number of unbounded problems they confront during the school day. If teachers make decisions about curriculum at all, they may choose to dispense with them easily by defining them narrowly, as bounded problems. In so doing they ignore the fact that most curriculum problems can be defined in several ways. They also ignore the fact that they, as teachers, are often the most qualified to address curriculum issues in the manner that best serves their students. Consider this example suggested by a reading of Goodman (1988).

Suppose a highly centralized school district appoints district-wide curriculum committees to decide on materials and objectives for each subject and each grade level. In response to the committee's recommendations, the district purchases comprehensive instructional programs for reading and language arts that will prepare students for the state-mandated standardized reading and writing tests. The programs contain lists of specific performance objectives, step-by-step procedures for teaching, time schedules, and tests. These programs seem to facilitate the process of instruction and are extremely convenient for teachers to use. Teachers need not agonize over what reading materials are best for students, how to organize the language arts activities, or how to evaluate the effects of the instructional process.

Given all of their other duties, from collecting lunch money to meeting with parents, most teachers view the lack of autonomy in producing the language arts curriculum as a blessing. They readily accept the judgment of the curriculum committees, whose sole mission was to make the best decisions on curriculum matters. The teachers' reaction is an understandable response to the realities of the structure of the school as a workplace.

But one teacher in the district, Noriko Chiba, is not at peace with herself after several weeks of using the new curriculum. As an inquiring, reflective teacher who cares about her students' successful learning experiences, Ms. Chiba has doubts about the language arts program. She has noticed that many of her students are bored with the skill pack, and even her academically capable pupils resist using the study book. Disturbed by her own lack of enthusiasm—which she attempts to disguise with feigned buoyancy—when teaching language arts, Ms. Chiba questions the long-term educational value of using these materials. "What good is it to be a skillful reader if one is also joyless and alienated from the reading process?" she asks herself. "Will my students, even the bright ones, hesitate to read on their own if they equate reading with drudgery?"

Unlike her colleagues who accept the packaged program, Ms. Chiba chooses to define the question of the language arts curriculum as an unbounded problem. Suddenly the issue is no longer limited to the relatively manageable, technical decision as to how best to impart predetermined skills. Now the curricular question is a social, moral, and even a political issue. It is social because this inquiring teacher is honoring the values, feelings, and interests of her students instead of accepting, without reflection, the beliefs, values, and goals of her superiors. It is moral because, in attending to her own educational values, beliefs, and goals, Ms. Chiba is confronting the ethical issue of whether she is mis-educating her students and turning them off to reading for the sake of convenience. And finally, in questioning the legitimacy of the curriculum decisions made for her, she is engaging in thinking which, if acted upon, will have political consequences.

Rejecting all or part of the mandated materials would place Ms. Chiba at odds with her superiors. Varying degrees of resistance on her part are possible. For example, she could attempt to negotiate quietly behind the scenes with her superiors, hoping for a morally acceptable compromise. She could openly crusade for support from her colleagues in an attempt to overturn the committees' decision. She could find the situation morally intolerable and seek alternate employment in a setting that offers her more curricular autonomy.

Whatever course she chooses, Ms. Chiba has become a curriculum leader by opening the boundaries that framed this particular curriculum problem. She has chosen to honor in a responsible fashion her own deeply held professional views on what should be taught and how.

Building a Curriculum Platform

The sum of an individual's beliefs concerning curriculum development constitute what Walker (1971) has called a *curriculum platform.* Walker explains:

> The word platform is meant to suggest both a political platform and something to stand on. The platform includes an idea of what is and a vision of what ought to be, and these guide the curriculum developer in determining what he should do to realize his vision. (p. 75)

The pursuit of this vision must, of course, be tempered with an appreciation of what is realistically attainable. Extreme idealists do not last long in the teaching profession, nor perhaps in any other corner of the real world. But curriculum leaders are willing to think critically about teaching practices and to challenge, when necessary, the mandates supporting them.

The alternative is to engage in the kind of uncritical acceptance of school practices that Katz (1974) called *excessive realism.* Excessive realists consistently avoid seeing curriculum and other educational issues as unbounded problems that are social, moral, or political in nature. Instead they accept standardized practices as representing "the limits of what is possible" (Goodman, 1988). When what *is* obscures what *could be,* and *limits* replace *visions,* a curriculum platform becomes simply a mirror of the present.

Whether or not a teacher challenges the status quo, his or her curriculum platform has three important dimensions: *content selection, content organization,* and *evaluation.* Each dimension encompasses numerous questions that can be answered in many different ways.

Platform Dimension #1: Content Selection

What knowledge is of most worth? Educational philosophers, curriculum theorists, and teachers have long wondered about *what* students should be learning. Clearly not everything can be taught in school. What, then, are the criteria by which educational content should be prioritized?

This platform dimension is even more complex than it initially appears. It invites a series of additional questions. For example, should there be a universal curriculum for all students in a society or in an individual classroom, regardless of interests, propensities, socioeconomic background, and so on? Should content be sorted out according to disciplines and subject areas, or should student learning be comprised of trans-disciplinary content that focuses on "real world" problems? Should the curriculum completely avoid teaching content in the usual sense and, instead, impart critical thinking skills that can be applied to a wide range of problems? Should students be taught the content, skills, attitudes, and behavioral norms needed to merely survive in the real world, or should they be emotionally and intellectually primed to change the world for the better? Should values and attitudes be taught at all in school? Can schools avoid teaching them? Should they be a part of the overt, "advertised" curriculum, or should schools teach them covertly, as part of the "hidden" curriculum?

Such questions raise the fundamental issue of where educators should look to find the legitimate source of educational content and curriculum goals that are of most worth. Should subject matter experts hand teachers the curriculum in each discipline? Or should folks in the local community be surveyed to ascertain the desired curriculum content? Perhaps teachers should observe and listen to their students to derive goals from their interests and needs. Or should teachers conjure up a vision of what the citizens of a more just and humane world would be like, and aim the educational process in that direction?

Platform Dimension #2: Content Organization

The second dimension of a curriculum platform concerns the organization of curriculum content. Some curriculum developers consider questions about organization only after the content has been selected. They regard it as a matter of effectively sequencing the content that has already been selected by the curriculum designer, whether that be the teacher or an external source. Members of this group advocate lists of performance objectives to be shared with students at the outset of a learning activity. This list serves to tightly organize the instructional process in advance.

Other curriculum developers believe that the curriculum should not be organized in advance of the act of teaching. Instead they prefer to let the curriculum unfold as the student interacts with the learning environment. They believe that a structure emerges during a dynamic learning process, and that this process will be stultified if content is precisely determined in advance. This group suggests a general outline of content that allows useful tangents, serendipitous events, or "teachable moments" to be seized upon and used effectively.

The issue here is one of control. The first group, advocates of teacher-centered curricula, attempts to maximally control the content to be learned. In this approach instruction occurs only after decisions about content selection and organization have been finalized. The second group, advocates of student-centered curricula, encourage self-propelled involvement in individual and group-oriented activities, and de-emphasize a teacher-imposed curriculum. This group tends to minimize any distinction between curriculum and teaching.

Numerous related issues arise within this dimension of curriculum problem solving. In a teacher-centered curriculum, for example, what are some effective strategies for logically sequencing material to be learned? Is there one best way of doing this? How should one's goals or objectives be formulated? What purposes do they serve? In a student-centered approach, how might the learning environment be arranged to entice students into having worthwhile experiences? What are some strategies for curriculum planning that honor student interests and needs while guiding them through educational activities?

Platform Dimension #3: Evaluation

A third dimension of curriculum problem solving concerns evaluation. While some educators believe that evaluation lies outside of the purview of the curriculum, the authors agree with Zumwalt (1989) that

> an understanding of the role of evaluation in the designing and redesigning of curriculum . . . is central for the professional teacher who has the autonomy and responsibility to reflect and deliberate about curriculum. (p. 174)

The increasing tendency of agencies outside of the classroom and school to mandate evaluation in the form of standardized tests places limits on that autonomy. Here, perhaps more than in other dimensions, teachers are pressured to view the problems of evaluation as bounded rather than unbounded. For example, when teachers are formally or informally evaluated on the basis of their students' standardized test scores, they may be tempted to teach directly to these tests, substituting them for the curriculum. Under these circumstances questions concerning the first dimension, what knowledge is of most worth, become moot. The only remaining questions are technical ones about which methods of instruction will maximize students' test-taking proficiencies.

For inquiring teachers who refuse to see the issues of evaluation as bounded, however, other complex questions arise. What should be the relationship, if any, between my goals and the tests I give to my students? What are some effective techniques for creating teacher-made tests? What are the ramifications of equating evaluation with testing? What are some alternative approaches to assessing student learning besides testing? How do I evaluate for change and growth in students' interests and values? Should I attempt to evaluate for "incidental learnings," those learnings that are difficult to predict in advance of an educational activity? If so, how can I do this?

An inquiring, reflective teacher faces a plethora of questions about each dimension of the curriculum platform. Many of these questions may not have final, correct answers, but will require continual reexamination throughout one's teaching career. The four historically significant teacher-characters advocate specific positions with regard to classroom curriculum leadership questions that may help you refine your own curriculum platform.

TEACHER INSIGHTS

Johnny Jackson

I have some very specific ideas about the three important dimensions of curriculum leadership. First, the issue of what knowledge is of most worth. I believe that our duty as teachers is to renew within the next generation the cultural heritage that we ourselves have inherited. The acquisition of this cultural heritage, the accumulated wisdom of past generations, empowers our students, for with it they need not go about reinventing the wheel, rediscovering for themselves every important skill or piece of time-tested information. The most important aspects of this heritage are embodied within the academic disciplines that are usually—and rightfully—taught in school.

Each of the disciplines is comprised of an important group of canonical works. These are works of science, literature, art, and so on, that have stood the test of time and are valued by the experts within each field. As a high school English teacher, I believe students should confront classical works of literature, those which a consensus of scholars consider highly meritorious. For example, in 1984 the chairman of the National Endowment for the Humanities, William Bennett, surveyed scholars, journalists, teachers, and government leaders to determine which texts should be studied in school. The literary works cited most often included *Macbeth, Hamlet,* and Twain's *Huckleberry Finn* ("U.S. culture," 1984). I think these are excellent choices. Most textbooks on the market are developed under the guidance of renowned scholars and are good sources of content in literature and in the other disciplines.

This leads me to the question of curriculum organization. Each discipline seems to have a logical order in which the content is already arranged. For example, when teaching history it seems appropriate to sequence the material chronologically. Students vicariously relive historical events in the order in which they occurred, and they construct new learning on their already existing knowledge base. Similarly, when teaching mathematics, following the logical progression of the discipline would mean building from simple skills to the more complex. Posner and Rudnitsky (1982) write: "If it can be determined empirically that the learning of one skill facilitates the learning of a subsequent skill, the first skill can be termed an empirical prerequisite of the second" (p. 114).

You must also consider a second facet of this process of organizing curriculum content: the experiential and developmental readiness of the student to internalize this content, to make it truly her own. Unless the teacher knows how to build a bridge between the world of academic knowledge and the experiential world of the student, only superficial, detached learning takes place. The student must also learn to appreciate and cherish what it is that she has learned. As a hero of mine, R. S. Peters (1964), has argued, education can be seen as a process in which a teacher initiates a student into the "citadel" of existing knowledge.

> One technique of initiation is . . . to lure people inside the citadel by using their existing interests in the hope that, once inside, they will develop other interests which previously were never dreamed of. . . . This is, of course, a very limited conception of initiation. For it neglects the fluidity of wants. What people in fact want or are interested in is, to a large extent, a product of their previous initiation. The job of the educator is not simply to build on existing wants but to present what is worth wanting in such a way that it creates new wants and stimulates new interests. (p. 45)

Think back to your own experiences as a student in school. Who were the teachers who taught you the most about the larger culture while increasing your interest in it? Did you have an English teacher who initiated you into the splendors of Latin while engendering enthusiasm and respect for this language? Did you have a science teacher who made you want to learn more about the relationships among scientific concepts?

Recall the example I cited in chapter 3 of an English teacher who introduces *Julius Caesar* by way of *Star Trek.* That teacher is a master at introducing important content in an engaging way. As he travels with his students through that story with its own internal structure, he continues to build bridges between Shakespeare's ideas and his students' lives. For such a teacher, organizing the curriculum means respecting the internal structure within each discipline, but teaching it in a way that makes students want to discover more about the knowledge that constitutes our cultural heritage.

Finally, what about evaluation? Evaluation serves as the means for determining our students' level of cultural literacy. Tests and exams should, therefore, focus on information with which all of our students should be intimately acquainted. You may determine whether your teacher-made tests are aligned with this content by consulting works such as Hirsch's (1989) *The Dictionary of Cultural Literacy.* In this book is distilled the core content of the culture. However, I also recommend that you foster your students' multicultural literacy. Their core reading list should include classics from a variety of intellectual traditions: African-American, Native American, Hispanic, and so on.

Simonson and Walker's *The Gray Wolf Annual 5: A Multi-Cultural Literacy* (1988) is a good curriculum reference for this topic. This book includes selections from the works of James Baldwin, Paula Gunn Allen, Carlos Fuentes, and other great writers.

We must take care when evaluating our students that we are not merely asking them to give back the results of rote memorization. We must insist that they *internalize* the information and ideas in the curriculum. Our tests and exams should be constructed to ascertain whether they have processed and played with these Great Thoughts. It is difficult, if not impossible, to do this using objective tests with their multiple-choice, matching, or true-false questions. Essay exams and papers, on the other hand, require students to synthesize or evaluate what they have learned. Certainly they also mean more work for the teacher because they take more time to grade, but look at the rewards! If each American teacher would consistently teach and evaluate important content in this manner, the sorry tales of cultural illiteracy among American students would fade away.

Susan Smith

I urge you to take an efficient, systematic, and analytical approach to constructing a classroom curriculum. My method, which is based on Tyler's (1949) famous rationale for curriculum development, consists of five distinct steps.

1. Identify the instructional objectives.
2. Perform a task analysis and use the results to sequence the objectives.
3. Share the objectives with your students.
4. Instruct so as to facilitate accomplishment of these objectives.
5. Use the list of objectives as a guide in developing good evaluation instruments.

Let us begin with the identification of goals or objectives. I believe that both teacher and students must be crystal clear about what is to be taught and learned before starting a classroom activity. This means that the classroom curriculum leader must (a) decide upon the most appropriate desired learning outcomes, (b) carefully formulate them as instructional objectives, and (c) share these with students as a device for organizing the learning activity in advance, so that everyone knows precisely where she or he is heading.

Where should the objectives come from? The teacher should be the one who ultimately selects appropriate objectives for the student. But the teacher is also part of a larger organizational team attempting to impart information to students as efficiently as possible. Duplication of, and gaps in, necessary content and skills must be avoided. Therefore local school districts, state departments of education, or even committees of teachers in individual schools often prepare content in the form of lists of objectives, skills, or competencies. Items on these lists are parceled out to teachers according to grade levels and courses of study. Using the lists allows teachers and students to see their efforts in one course or grade level as part of a larger project for which the overall learning outcomes have been carefully articulated.

TenBrink (1986) has identified other important sources of instructional objectives for use especially when no lists like those described above are available to a teacher. One source is published teaching resources such as textbooks, workbooks, educational games, and audio-visual materials. Another source is other teachers in the same subject area or grade level. Professional journals often include lists of objectives in articles about successful units of instruction.

In gathering or composing a list of objectives, I believe that it is important to pay attention to form. The form that the objectives take will determine the probability of the instructor successfully communicating to the students her instructional intent. Objectives must be meaningfully stated. Although a variety of formats are used for writing objectives, my favorite is Mager's (1962) approach. Mager suggests that writing a meaningfully stated objective involves three steps:

> First, identify the terminal behavior by name; you can specify the kind of behavior that will be accepted as evidence that the learner has achieved the objective. Second, try to define the desired behavior further by describing the important conditions under which the behavior will be expected to occur. Third, specify the criteria of acceptable performance by describing how well the learner must perform to be considered acceptable. (1962, p. 12)

Here is an example of a meaningfully stated objective to be shared with students at the beginning of a learning exercise:

> When asked to write a short paper explaining the methodologies of psychological research, the student should be able to use correctly 10 out of 15 major concepts that were presented in class lecture (TenBrink, 1986, p. 107).

The terminal behavior here is the correct use of methodologies of psychological research. The conditions under which the behavior should occur are those of writing a short paper. The acceptable performance level is 10 out of 15 of the concepts presented.

I recommend that you consult Mager's book and practice writing good behavioral objectives.

Once you have formulated your list of objectives, you need to sequence them effectively. Task analysis is an interesting approach to sequencing objectives. It is a process that breaks down complex learning behaviors into component parts. The teacher analyzes a task to describe precisely the steps or links in the "behavioral chain" and their proper sequence (Alberto & Troutman, 1982). Each step should be simple enough for students to master without great difficulty. Steps can be written in the form of objectives and should be logically sequenced from basic to complex.

Let me illustrate my point with an easy-to-understand example taken from primary education. The task of reading readiness can be broken down into the following sequence of skills:

1. Students should practice visual perception. Students should be able to discriminate shapes, such as triangles from squares, and letter shapes, such as *A* from *H*.
2. Students should be able to discriminate among different sounds, such as various farm animals.
3. Students should identify the upper-case letters.
4. Students should identify the lower-case letters.
5. Students should make the letter sounds, such as short and long vowels.
6. Students should blend sounds together, such as *cat, sat, mat.*
7. Students should read sight words, such as *the, and*, and *look.*

The instructional process follows this sequence. After one level of content has been mastered, the learner proceeds to the next, more complex level of performance. Task analysis is thus part of a teaching-learning approach in which students gradually master, one at a time, a set of increasingly challenging objectives or intended learning outcomes.

How do we know which students have achieved which objectives? To evaluate students' mastery of curriculum content, we need a test that explicitly relates what is being measured to what has been taught. This kind of test is called a *criterion-referenced test.* In answering specific items on such a test, students get "relevant, on-target practice in the skills or knowledge being taught" (Popham, 1987, p. 16). For example, items on a reading test should correspond to each of the subskills identified above. This enables the teacher to identify and record precisely which skills each student has and has not mastered.

Constructing good tests is a complex process that I cannot describe in detail here. I recommend that you take a course in your preservice program to help you become a good test-maker. You may also want to consult Gronlund (1985) for helpful advice on evaluation and test-making.

Dennis Sage

The process of curriculum development is, to me, a very personal one, and the relevant persons include both the teacher and the students. Students' real needs and interests are often ignored in curriculum-making, but teachers have a moral obligation to consider those needs. I agree with the humanistic psychologists that each child has a number of internal needs that must be kept in balance. When these needs are out of balance, the child feels a desire to do something that will return her to a state of equilibrium.

According to Abraham Maslow (1954), the highest or most complex need is the need for self-actualization. Self-actualization is the attainment of one's innate potential. To be self-actualized is thus to have become all one can be, a unique and fulfilled human being who sees her or his life as meaningful.

The curriculum must aim to fulfill each student's need for self-actualization. By definition, then, the curriculum must be different for each student. Moreover, the emergence of needs and desires is an ongoing process, making them difficult to predict in advance. In addition, because a human being is a growing, changing organism, all of these needs are interrelated in a complex web, each continually affecting the others.

Because of the personal, dynamic, and holistic character of student needs, I reject the use of behavioral performance objectives in teaching. Objectives are standardized, they are formulated prior to learning engagements, and they attempt to divide learning up into discrete behavioral particles. They do not reflect the true diversity of human needs.

But how does one teacher, in the confines of a self-contained classroom, cope with the individual needs of 23 student-organisms? Let me recommend the ideas of two educators, Herbert Kohl and Kieran Egan. Kohl (1976) suggests a thematic or web approach to developing lessons. There are three steps in this approach, but it is not as sequential and inflexible as the one Susan Smith recommended.

The first step is to identify a curriculum theme that fulfills two important requirements: It should be intrinsically interesting to students, and it should be broad enough to allow a variety of activities to flow from it. Kohl uses the example of the circus as a theme for elementary school students.

> I chose this theme because the circus is magic to almost all of us. It combines danger and discipline, involves encountering and taming the wild and at times death itself, and combines farce and high seriousness. It encompasses so many different aspects of life and fantasy that it is very rare to find a student completely indifferent to the circus. (p. 30)

The second step is to cluster ideas into a web of subthemes. With "circus" in the center of the cluster, Kohl now draws lines outward to represent the following subthemes: clowns, tightrope walkers, animals, posters, art and music, and so on.

The third step is to further develop the subthemes, but now in terms of ideas for potential classroom activities. Here are just two of Kohl's examples of related activities for the subtheme of tightrope walking or balancing.

> Talking about fear of heights. How does feeling about the performance affect the performance? Maybe you could get into the whole question of confidence here. You can think up a number of writing topics dealing with times students were confident and times they were afraid.
>
> You can also measure the actual heights of the tightwire, and look at the differences in the low and high wires. And you can measure the heights the students are used to climbing. This may be a good way of studying the question of height in general. (pp. 34–35)

This kind of curriculum planning is best used in an open classroom setting. Ideally, to meet the dynamic personal needs of each child, a variety of projects should be available at any given time. An effective teacher knows intuitively how to entice each individual student into a meaningful educational experience that is personalized to his or her unique interests and abilities. Teachers may need to set up learning centers in various parts of the room, so that students can engage in flexible, personal, self-directed learning. Think about the hidden agenda of schools, especially high schools, that are organized like factories, with self-contained classrooms, high student-teacher ratios, desks in neat rows, etc. This rigid, compartmentalized organization makes it difficult to institute a flexible, dynamic, student-centered curriculum. Attempting to do so in this environment will present you with a highly unbounded problem indeed!

Egan (1985) offers a compromise solution to this problem. While certainly not perfect, his suggestions can allow for an acceptable degree of personalization and flexibility in the curriculum. Egan suggests that we think of a unit of the curriculum "as a story that is to be told, rather than as a set of objectives to be attained" (p. 401). He uses an exemplary unit on Native North Americans to illustrate the steps in his approach to curriculum development.

Egan suggests the teacher first identify an important, personally engaging topic for the unit (e.g., Native American life, for North American fifth graders). The next step follows from Egan's observation that most good children's stories are structured by "binary opposites," which are opposing concepts such as good and evil, bravery and cowardice, or fear and security. Egan suggests that the curriculum be told as a story structured around such binary opposites. For example, in Egan's unit on Native American culture, he suggests the binary opposites of survival and destruction. The third step is to organize the content of the story around the interplay of the two concepts:

> We could begin with a dramatic account of Plains Indians hunting; they took a food supply that could last for three days and it is the third day; the hunters grow weak, the village waits for fresh meat—what will happen? (Egan, 1985, p. 402)

The fourth step is to bring the story to a denouement or conclusion. The dramatic conflict inherent in the binary opposites is resolved or moved toward mediation. In the Native American unit one could develop the concept of equilibrium between culture and environment to show how cultures can, to some degree, accommodate to unstable environments. Participating in this particular story may help students understand why flexible cultures are better poised to deal with environmental threats and instability than inflexible ones.

I endorse Egan's storytelling approach, but with some reservations. The stories we tell as the curriculum need to be, in large part, our *students'* stories. Lest they adopt a passive posture toward the curriculum, students need to be tellers as well as listeners. If Egan's approach can insure that students actively share what they have learned, then I am all for it.

Finally, let me say something about evaluation. Evaluation is a vital classroom activity, but I deplore the fact that many people, both educators and non-educators, equate evaluation with testing. Like many other progressive thinkers (Barth, 1972; Gardner, 1967; Morrison, 1966; Silberman, 1970), I believe that objective tests trivialize and dehumanize the learning process. We need evaluation techniques that respect the complex, personal, dynamic nature of the curriculum process at its best. What are some alternative approaches? I suggest reading *Beyond Standardized Testing,* a booklet by Archbald and Newmann (1988). Although directed toward secondary schools, the booklet details a variety of novel, sensible techniques to evaluate academic achievement that are appropriate for most grade levels. I especially like the suggestions about exhibitions of student performances (p. 20) and portfolios of student works (pp. 29–30).

Sylvia Rivera

In chapter 4 I spoke of the need for transformative education that enables students to discover their role in creating a more just, humane, democratic society. Curriculum problem solving is critical to this transformative process. A classroom curriculum leader must possess a platform that (a) honors the possibility of a better world, (b) understands how to move beyond the prevailing social/political/economic system that impedes the realization of that world, and (c) suggests how to pass these attitudes and understandings on to her students.

Therefore my answer to the question "what knowledge is of most worth?" is this: It is that knowledge which enables each student to move beyond a state of subjugation toward a true mastery, or empowerment, over the affairs of her own life as part of a larger communal life. A good curriculum draws its content from those skills and domains of learning that foster this movement.

One public school program that offers students truly important skills and content is the Community Issues Program (CIP) implemented by Newmann, Bertocci, and Landsness (1977) in Madison, Wisconsin. The sequence of courses in this program includes these:

First semester:	Community service internship Political-legal process course Communications course
Second semester:	Citizens action project Action in literature project Public message

In the community service internship students contribute to the missions of governmental and social agencies and public interest organizations. Students volunteer in various capacities. They may aid a television news reporter, tutor young children, assist the elderly, or gather data for a neighborhood organization. In the political-legal process course students examine the formal and informal structure of the political system by analyzing the institutional processes they experienced in their internship. The language skills of the communications course are practiced in discussions and interviews with the people in these agencies and organizations.

In the second semester students are immersed in community affairs. The citizens action project, such as lobbying for legislation and establishing special youth institutions, usually develops from the first semester's internship. Students attend clinics on political and social skills such as fund raising and canvassing techniques while developing their project. Meanwhile students read critical works of drama, poetry, biography, and fiction by writers such as Gandhi, Thoreau, and James Baldwin in the action in literature project. The discussions that grow out of these texts challenge students to confront issues of political struggle, civil disobedience, and the nature of the "good society." Finally, in the public message course, students communicate their experiences and discoveries in the program to the general public.

This curriculum moves out of the sheltered, artificial, naive world of the self-contained classroom into the realities of public life. I believe that this kind of curriculum is crucial to the progressive education of future citizens. A community-based curriculum is more difficult to implement with younger children, but a transformative educational approach can also be used in an elementary school setting. Adler and Goodman (1986) offer several suggestions for activities that promote a "critical pedagogy" for teaching history for younger kids:

1. Students "do" history rather than "learn about" historical events. For example, "children examine history through photographs, artifacts, and oral reporting of past events" and then "attempt to portray what life might have been like during a given historical event or period of time" (p. 5). This requires that children imagine, speculate, and analyze rather than merely memorize.

2. Students view slides of turn-of-the-century transportation systems and then watch demonstrations of various types of shaving razors. Students are encouraged to speculate about the "materials, design, function, and values (e.g., disposability, efficiency, safety, materialism) that played a role in the development" (p. 5) of each.

3. After reading biographical sketches of life in Wisconsin between 1880 and 1940, students use various historical themes (e.g., food, clothing, housing, occupations, entertainment, social roles, families) to analyze the life of the individuals portrayed.

Teachers must learn to see all learning as value based, not as a set of skills or content that is taught in a moral vacuum. Even our teaching methods have half-hidden consequences, which makes it unwise to think of curriculum and instruction as two separate processes. Moffett (1985), for example, decried methods of teaching reading that treat texts as meaningless word particles or isolated words rather than as potentially powerful tools. The use of phonics or atomistically programmed workbooks tends to render reading insipid. Such methods appear to teach reading while actually crippling it, never allowing students to see "reading as a personal resource with which to do what *they* want to do" (p. 53). Thus such pedagogical approaches implicitly value *a*literacy and the disempowerment of students over their own lives. The whole language approach and Freire's (1972) social literacy training approach, on the other hand, help students to associate reading with an exploration of their own values and their connections with the larger world.

We need to sequence our curriculum content in a manner that continuously entices students to make these associations and connections. Note the strategy used in the CIP program. In the first semester students become acquainted with an intrinsically interesting community-based activity and acquire communications skills at least partially within this real world context. The second semester is designed to increase student mastery of knowledge and skills. Seizing on their students' enthusiasm for the citizens action projects, the curriculum leaders provide access to relevant readings and discussions. These help students make connections between their work and the struggles of others attempting to improve life in other contexts.

Evaluation strategies need, likewise, to be carefully selected. We teachers must avoid giving students the sense that artificial rewards such as good grades or honor rolls are the primary reason for learning. In the CIP, Newmann recommends using evaluation as a tool for giving students critical feedback on their work and as an opportunity for assessing the meaningfulness of their projects in terms of their own lives. For only if students become interested in and capable at working toward a more just and peaceful world can we say that our curriculum leadership has been successful. Newmann seems to understand what education *should* be about.

Personal-Professional Inquiry

In chapter 3 you studied five categories of constructivist learning questions: remembered anecdotes, role models, personal metaphors, community referents, and teacher-characters' discourse. Now you will explore four of these categories with reference to the topic of curriculum leadership.

1. Describe any past experiences you have had in making decisions about curricula. Were these decisions bounded or unbounded decisions? In what ways? Were any of the experiences positive ones? What was positive about them? Were any of the experiences negative ones? What was negative about them?
2. Describe a teacher who was a positive role model for making wise curriculum decisions. Why was this person a positive role model? Have you experienced a negative role model? Describe why that person was a negative role model.
3. Using the term "curriculum leadership" as your nucleus, create a cluster. Select a personal metaphor from your cluster and compose a paragraph that explores what that metaphor means to you.
4. a. Think about one unit of content or a topic that you expect to teach in the future. Tell whether each teacher-character would include or reject that unit or topic. Explain the reasoning behind each decision.
   b. Make a rough sketch of how each of the teacher-characters might sequence the content within that unit.
   c. How would each evaluate the learning that has taken place?
5. What other questions occur to you as you inquire into curriculum leadership?

Further Readings

The following books will help you learn more about curriculum leadership. You can study these books independently or as part of a course.

Alberto, P. A., & Troutman, A. C. (1982). *Applied behavior analysis for teachers: Influencing student performance* (2nd ed.). Columbus, OH: Merrill.

Archbald, D. A., & Newmann, F. M. (1988). *Beyond standardized testing: Assessing authentic academic achievement in the secondary school.* Reston, VA: National Association of Secondary School Principals.

Egan, K. (1985). *Teaching as storytelling.* Chicago: University of Chicago Press.

Eisner, E. (1986). *The educational imagination.* New York: Macmillan.

Gronlund, N. E. (1985). *Measurement and evaluation in teaching* (5th ed.). New York: Macmillan.

Kohl, H. (1976). *On teaching.* New York: Schocken.

Mager, R. F. (1962). *Preparing instructional objectives.* Belmont, CA: Fearon.

Newmann, F. W., Bertocci, T., & Landsness, R. M. (1977). *Skills in citizen action: An English-social studies program for secondary schools.* Skokie, IL: National Textbook.

Posner, G., & Rudnitsky, A. N. (1982). *Course design: A guide to curriculum development for teachers* (2nd ed.). New York: Longman.

TenBrink, T. D. (1986). Writing instructional objectives. In J. M. Cooper (Ed.), *Classroom teaching skills* (pp. 67–110). Lexington, MA: D.C. Heath.

References

Adler, S., & Goodman, J. (1986). Critical theory as a foundation for methods courses. *Journal of Teacher Education, 37*(4), 2–8.

Alberto, P. A., & Troutman, A. C. (1982). *Applied behavior analysis for teachers: Influencing student performance* (2nd ed.). Columbus, OH: Merrill.

Archbald, D. A., & Newmann, F. M. (1988). *Beyond standardized testing: Assessing authentic academic achievement in the secondary school.* Reston, VA: National Association of Secondary School Principals.

Barth, R. S. (1972). *Open education and the American school.* New York: Schocken.

Egan, K. (1985). Teaching as storytelling: A non-mechanistic approach to planning teaching. *Journal of Curriculum Studies, 17*(4), 397–406.

Freire, P. (1972). *The pedagogy of the oppressed.* New York: Herder and Herder.

Gardner, D. E. (1967). *Does progressive primary education work?* London: Association for Childhood Education International.

Goodman, J. (1988). The political and teaching strategies of reflective, active preservice teachers. *Elementary School Journal, 89*(1), 25–40.

Gronlund, N. E. (1985). *Measurement and evaluation in teaching* (5th ed.). New York: Macmillan.

Hirsch, E. D. (1989). *The dictionary of cultural literacy: What every American needs to know.* Boston: Houghton Mifflin.

Katz, L. (1974). Issues and problems in teacher education. In B. Spodek (Ed.), *Teacher education: Of the teacher, by the teacher, for the child* (pp. 1–19). Washington D.C.: National Association for Education of Young Children.

KOHL, H. (1976). *On teaching*. New York: Schocken.

MAGER, R. F. (1962). *Preparing instructional objectives*. Belmont, CA: Fearon.

MASLOW, A. H. (1954). *Motivation and personality*. New York: Harper & Row.

MOFFETT, J. (1985). Hidden impediments to improving English teaching. *Phi Delta Kappan, 67*(1), 50–56.

MORRISON, P. (1966). Tensions of purpose. [Special issue]. *ESI Quarterly Report, 2*.

NEWMANN, F. W., BERTOCCI, T., & LANDSNESS, R. M. (1977). *Skills in citizen action: An English-social studies program for secondary schools*. Skokie, IL: National Textbook.

PETERS, R. S. (1964). *Education as initiation*. London: Lowe & Brydone.

POPHAM, W. J. (1987). Instructional objectives benefit teaching and testing. *Momentum, 28*(2), 15–16.

POSNER, G., & RUDNITSKY, A. N. (1982). *Course design: A guide to curriculum development for teachers* (2nd ed.). New York: Longman.

SILBERMAN, C. E. (1970). *Crisis in the classroom: The remaking of American education*. New York: Random House.

SIMONSON, R., & WALKER, S. (Eds.). 1988. Opening the American mind [Special issue]. *The Gray Wolf Annual, 5*.

TENBRINK, T. D. (1986). Writing instructional objectives. In J. M. Cooper (Ed.), *Classroom teaching skills* (pp. 67–110) Lexington, MA: D.C. Heath.

TYLER, R. (1949). *Basic principles of curriculum and instruction*. Chicago: University of Chicago Press.

U.S. culture czar lists must-reads. (1984, August 12). *Cincinnati Enquirer*, p. A–8.

WALKER, D. F. (1971). A naturalistic model for curriculum development. *School Review, 80*(1), 51–69.

ZUMWALT, K. (1989). Beginning professional teachers: The need for a curricular vision of teaching. In M. C. Reynolds (Ed.), *Knowledge base for the beginning teacher* (pp. 173–184). Oxford: Pergamon Press.

CHAPTER 6

Inquiring into Classroom Community Leadership

Introduction

In this chapter you will examine a model of the classroom as a community with shared purposes, activities, norms, consequences and responsibilities. This view includes a picture of the student as a whole person who lives both inside and outside the walls of the school. Classroom community leadership will be seen as a deliberative process that involves establishing democratic community norms, analyzing and resolving disruptions to these norms, and facilitating student autonomy based on democratic values. The consideration of this three-part process naturally builds on chapter 4's focus on problem solving. The topic of curriculum leadership in chapter 5 is also closely related to the concept of classroom community leadership. If the learning activities are appropriate, relevant, and engaging, classroom management becomes less of an issue because the community of the classroom moves toward the shared purpose of learning.

Lortie (1975) notes that a student teacher coming into the classroom with 13,000 hours of experience as a student sees the classroom in terms of his or her own experience. We have all had experiences that predispose us to envision school as what we already know it to be. This seems to be especially true in terms of classroom management. Unfortunately "discipline" has come to mean control through punitive measures and autocratic authority. The people who are "disciplined," i.e., the students, are often left out of the processes of making and enforcing the rules. To inquire into the topic of classroom community leadership, you may have to suspend your notions of "discipline" and "management" and begin to develop new terms for the kinds of relationships that exist between adults and young people. You will have to expand your thinking about how caring professionals share space with the young people in their care.

The Classroom As a Democratic Learning Community

The model of the classroom as a "learning community" (Florio-Ruane, 1989, p. 167) in which the caring teacher is the leader begins with the ideas of shared purposes and mutual respect. It's described here in detail because it is the basic concept upon which everything else is built, and the norms which are established reflect its character. Every class begins as a group of students and a teacher who occupy a room in a school building for the purpose of education. Together they create a special and unique place. The teacher's task is to see that each class becomes a community in which learning takes place and growth and change are fostered.

Characteristics of the Classroom As a Democratic Learning Community

A positive learning environment is a physically and psychologically safe place in which trust and mutual respect exist among all the members. Physical, verbal, and psychological abuse have no place in a nurturing environment. Students should not feel threatened, maligned, inferior, or inadequate. Each day students should enter the classroom with expectations of success and leave it with feelings of satisfaction and accomplishment.

Teachers who exercise democratic classroom leadership seize all opportunities to foster a trusting social environment. Their primary focus is on the quality of the relationships they have with their students, not on any particular authoritative role they have established. They understand that they must teach trusting community values in all kinds of circumstances. Wayson (1984) says that

> true teaching occurs in the hallway conversations, on the playground, during home visits, in the after class conversations teachers hold when they "are not teaching" . . . whenever the teacher and the student can interact with one another as human beings and not within the confines of institutionalized roles. These informal activities . . . are essential for

> building the trust and confidence necessary for an individual to accept and assimilate academic information from another. (p. 1232)

Cooperation is an integral part of daily living in a democratic learning community. All the students and the adults who inhabit it feel a sense of ownership because they have investments in and are part of the decision making that goes on there. Decisions must be worthwhile and important to the group, not throwaways that have no real significance. Consensus and cooperation are not easily achieved, but teachers must recognize them as fundamental classroom goals that are essential to the curriculum as well as to daily life outside the classroom.

One way teachers can achieve these goals is by setting up cooperative learning experiences that require students to help and teach each other. In this way teachers promote peer collaboration rather than peer competition. Teachers explicitly direct and discuss the relevance of respect for others and what fairness means.

Negotiation is another key element of the democratic learning community. Both learning and rules may be negotiated. Florio-Ruane (1989) says that "teachers do not control what is learned. Rather learning is negotiated or socially constructed by teachers and pupils as they communicate within broader contexts of education" (p. 166). Good teachers give up some of their authority in the classroom because they recognize that autonomy and the acquisition of self-control are significant aims of the educational process. Students need to be supported in their development toward independence. Much time and effort must be spent on nurturing those skills. Teachers must find ways to incorporate all this into the routines of the classroom. Florio-Ruane says that teachers need to

> create classroom communities in which the teachers' authority is sufficiently mitigated for students to learn freely, perhaps even joyously. This transformation occurs in such learning situations as (a) discussions which encourage student questioning and problem solving, (b) peer tutoring, (c) cooperative learning, (d) writing conferences. . . . In this kind of teaching, having acquired a sense of both the normative structure of schooling and one's option to improvise within it . . . teachers and students experience redefinition of their rights and obligations vis-à-vis one another and their academic work. (p. 166)

Activities such as discussions, peer tutoring, cooperative learning, and writing conferences promote members of the community working and moving together toward the common goal of education. The teacher realizes that he or she is not the only source of knowledge and establishes a learning environment in which students help each other construct knowledge in meaningful ways.

A Successful Democratic Learning Community: The Child Development Project

Schaps and Solomon (1990) describe a project that "fosters the creation of a caring community within each school and each classroom" (p. 38). The Child Development Project followed students from classrooms in which prosocial behavior was fostered and nurtured, teachers served as "values advocates," and justice, tolerance, and concern for others were common goals. All of the teachers involved incorporated developmental discipline, a literature-based approach to reading instruction, and cooperative learning into their classrooms.

DEVELOPMENTAL DISCIPLINE. Developmental discipline is a classroom management approach that involves the students in the governance of the classroom. Teachers share their authority with the students by discussing and jointly determining community norms and values and finding solutions for mutual problems. For example, students of any age could help develop a policy about homework. The goal would be for students to take responsibility to complete relevant homework independently. The entire process would be determined with input from the students. What kind of work should be given? Does it count toward the grade? What happens if students don't do it? Should it be done individually or in groups? How much time should it take? Does it always have to be written? There are no right or wrong ways to do homework; together the teacher and class select the alternatives that best suit their particular classroom community and academic goals.

THE LITERATURE-BASED APPROACH TO READING INSTRUCTION. The literature-based approach to reading helps motivate students to read and to learn how to read. It also helps students understand prosocial values and "how those values play out in real life" (Schaps & Solomon, 1990, p. 40). Students read a novel, for example, not only to understand plot and character but also to learn about norms and values that are an intrinsic part of literature and life. They have opportunities to reflect on meaningful events in their own lives and to experience the personal and cultural importance of good literature. They are not just rotely practicing reading skills but are seriously studying important aesthetic works.

COOPERATIVE LEARNING. Cooperative learning involves not only pairing students from the same classroom in learning activities, but also pairing students from other classrooms on projects such as reading books to each other, planting gardens, or raising money for the school. Evaluators of the Child Development program found that "the greater the sense of community among the students in a program class, the more favorable their outcomes on measures of prosocial values, helping conflict resolution skill . . . and intrinsic motivation" (Schaps & Solomon, 1990, p. 40). All aspects of students' development—intellectual, social, and moral—were positively affected. You will learn more about cooperative learning as it applies to teachers' professional development in chapter 7.

Establishing Democratically Shared Classroom Norms

A significant characteristic of classroom community leadership is democratically shared norms. These standards of behavior determine how the members of the community are expected to act. In a democratic classroom the norms for behavior are based on democratic ideals of "fairness, equality, justice, and the pursuit of the common good" (Encyclopaedia Britannica Corporation, 1990). Dreikurs (1982) stresses that the "teaching of discipline as a basic value is an ongoing process and is not to be resorted to only in times of stress and misbehavior" (p. 80). The teacher as the community leader sets the norms for the classroom community not in isolation, but in consideration of the larger school community, neighborhood, and city. The norms reflect democratic ideals that must be internalized by the students in every classroom. For example, this code of ethics includes mutual respect and equitable treatment.

Conflict often occurs when the larger society does not mirror these values. If, for example, mutual respect is not common in the larger school community, then this norm of conduct has to be discussed in the classroom community. But again, establishing rules of behavior has to be one of the teacher's major goals.

Teachers who become democratic community leaders must rethink both their own and their students' responsibilities. The democratic teacher does not abdicate authority or responsibility. Setting limits is necessary and helps students understand how far their choices really extend. Dreikurs (1982) says that "discipline in this sense means teaching the child that there are certain rules in life that people live by and that it is expected that the child will become accustomed to these rules and adopt them for his own" (p. 75). This applies to young adults as well. The teacher determines which rules are nonnegotiable (such as leaving the room without permission or hitting another student) and strictly enforces them. Other rules and the consequences for breaking them are determined and negotiated with students. The classroom norms are flexible and may be modified throughout the year.

Freedom to make choices is an important element of the democratic classroom. The learning environment is a place in which teachers and students can make responsible decisions for themselves that also affect others. But with freedom comes responsibility; freedom without responsibility leads to chaos. The learning environment needs order and direction. Young people and adults both have to "own" their actions and behaviors before they can become self-disciplined. Taking responsibility for behavior leads to self-discipline. Dreikurs (1982) summarizes the responsibilities of the students in the democratic community.

> If children (and young people) are to become autonomous adults, they must grow into independence by being encouraged to find their own solutions, to have creative ideas and independent views as well as to carry out assigned tasks. . . . They must have the freedom to be responsible for their choices and their behavior, to say what they are thinking, to have mutual respect and trust for each other, to analyze and to make decisions different from the pattern of the typical school. (p. 35)

The democratic classroom prepares students to become responsible, active citizens in a democratic society. The goals extend beyond the classroom into the community at large.

The teacher anticipates problems before they occur and plans accordingly. For example, transitions from one activity to another often create anxiety and confusion for everyone involved. The teacher must plan for transitions as carefully as for lessons. For example, what will make the students' transitions from home to school or from class to class smoother? The caring teacher always responds to and nurtures the development of the whole person while attending to each individual's needs. Teachers as community leaders strive to empower students to become independent, self-directing, self-disciplined, and responsible decision makers just as they themselves strive for these qualities in their own professional and personal lives.

Teaching Classroom Norms Democratically

Norms that are democratically shared must also be democratically taught. Teachers should model the norms so that students have a working example of how democratic classrooms function. In this model the teacher must help students take responsibility for their own actions and follow the established classroom community norms. For students to be self-directed, it is essential that the norms be clearly articulated. Because contemporary social norms vary widely, it becomes especially important to consciously determine what norms govern a particular classroom or school.

No behavioral norms can apply to everyone in all circumstances. "Proper" behaviors are often situationally determined; appropriate behavior varies from situation to situation. Our behavior in church is different from our behavior at a baseball game. Each setting requires us to exhibit the behavior appropriate for that place at that time. Self-discipline means knowing when and how to act in situationally appropriate ways.

If discipline has as its ultimate goal supporting young people's growth into autonomous decision makers who exercise self-control, then it is also:

> the ability to act contrary to a norm when it violates a higher ethic. The social unit is unlikely to reward such behavior. . . . That characteristic of self-discipline dispels any tendency to equate discipline with obedience. It requires the use of good judgment, courage, higher ethical processes, and a great deal of social responsibility even to the detriment of immediate self-interest. (Wayson, 1984, p. 228)

Educators prepare students not only to participate in a democratic society as responsible citizens, but also to respond to decisions involving higher values. The implied goal is that these young people will change society for the better, that they themselves will take on leadership roles.

Discipline is best taught by creating a normative environment—one that surrounds students with people who behave correctly and who help young people reflect on their "best behavior." The teachers "conduct themselves appropriately and responsibly, they accept responsibility for correcting violations of the accepted code, unless the code violates a higher ethic" (Wayson, 1984, p. 229). There can be no double standards for teachers and students; in a democratic environment, everyone has the same rights. Teachers have to redefine the role of privilege. If a community rule prohibits chewing gum during school hours, that rule applies to teachers as well as to students. One of the most powerful ways teachers can develop self-discipline in young people is, ironically, to pay equal attention to their own behavior. The old adage, "Do what I say, not what I do," has to be abandoned. Modeling by adults is a powerful means for a child or young adult to acquire and practice behavior (Bandura & Walters, 1963).

George Wood (1990) has studied classrooms in which teachers nurtured the skills and attitudes necessary for democratic life. He found that, although there are different ways to achieve this goal, such classrooms share common characteristics. First, all these teachers created communities within the institution of school, "for it is only within a community, not an institution, that we hold fast to such principles as working for the common good, empathy, equity and self-respect" (Wood, p. 33). In some of the schools, the traditional structure and organization were changed. For example, grouping students for instruction according to ability was eliminated. The second characteristic was that school work was purposeful. Students wanted to share their work because it was important and meaningful to them. The last characteristic was that these schools opened their doors to the outside world to "show their young people the needs and possibilities that will confront them when they leave school" (Wood, 1990, p. 36). Wood characterizes these schools as laboratories where democracy is experienced as opposed to observed; where it is alive rather than dead.

Dealing with Disruptions

Disruptions to the classroom community come from many different sources. Often they come from members who are unwilling or unable to contribute. Some members may have legitimate gripes about their experiences in the community. Techniques for dealing with these kinds of problems range from behavior modification and assertive discipline to therapeutic methods. You may want to consult some of these for detailed plans. It is important to remember, however, that some troubled youngsters need resources that you cannot provide; some engage in power struggles with adults, and some simply cannot be part of a loving, caring, purposeful community. In these circumstances teachers must collaborate with parents and other professionals to establish appropriate socialization activities.

Anticipating Disruptions

Some disruptions are caused by the school itself, such as office interruptions or bureaucratic demands. Again, these incidents have to be anticipated. What are the classroom routines for interruptions due to messages from outside the classroom? Do the students know what to do while they wait for you to complete the business? Do you expect them to sit quietly for variable periods of time, unable to talk or move? These problems are unbounded; therefore, they may have no definitive answers. But the reflective, inquiring teacher will try various ways to deal with them and will consult other members of the classroom community for contributions into the problem solving.

Another factor that may cause disruption is your disposition, personality, or mood for the day! On some days the students may seem more difficult to get along with because you did not get enough sleep, or because you didn't prepare for the activities of the day. These factors affect the larger picture of classroom management.

Responding to Disruptions

Teachers constantly make decisions about how to respond to students' behavior. Some decisions are easy, but others may be quite difficult. How will you, as the classroom community leader, respond to problematic situations in your classroom?

Here is a mental checklist that you can implement in a real-life situation. Although the checklist is presented as a step-by-step procedure, many of the steps would actually happen simultaneously.

Step 1
Identify the disruption.
The first step is to observe an incident and identify it as a problem. However, in order to label the incident, you have to consider the behavior in the context of your community's particular norms and practices. Your values and your students' values determine whether the behavior is acceptable or in violation of the community's rules.

Step 2
Assess the cause of the problem.
You must determine the cause of the behavior to begin to understand how to deal with it. Maybe the cause is related to problems in curriculum leadership, or to a conflict with the norms of the school or the community at large. Perhaps the individual child's personal problems cause the behavior.

Step 3
Act to solve the problem.
Stop the behavior immediately, especially if it puts anyone in danger. Remind students of the expected behavior in their community. Disruptions need to be handled in a way that helps students to internalize the norms. This may take more time than

just stopping the behavior and doling out punishments, but it is an essential step in helping the students to control and determine their own behaviors. Eventually this approach will save time because you won't have to mediate every situation.

Step 4

Determine the consequences.

Some behaviors may have the consequence built into them. For example, a student may carelessly use a piece of playground equipment and get hurt. Others may have consequences that have already been determined by the members of the community. A student who misuses playground equipment might be required to attend an afterschool safety class designed and taught by older students.

Let's apply this mental checklist to an example. Suppose a student is being confrontational with you over a homework assignment. Applying the first step of the checklist involves deciding that this is a disruption that needs your attention. Next you have to think about community norms. Does this incident violate those norms? In this case, the student is probably violating the norm concerning mutual respect and the rule about completing homework assignments.

Step 2 reminds you to look for the cause of the problem. You now have to take a step back to determine if the cause of the problem was in the assignment, and thus in the curriculum. Is this a curriculum problem rather than simply a behavior problem? If so, perhaps the student needs an opportunity to talk about the assignment.

In Step 3 you need to act. You may need to tell the student to immediately stop talking to you in a disrespectful manner. You may have to remind the members of the community of the norms they are responsible for maintaining. Perhaps the homework assignment should be changed or the student's ability to complete it should be determined.

Step 4 looks at the consequences, which need to be fair and related to the situation. They may include responding on a personal level instead of, or in addition to, on a formal, authoritative level. You may want to tell the student that you feel hurt by such unwarranted, negative comments. Perhaps you should schedule a conference with the student's parents to discuss the student's homework habits and difficulties. Looking at other ideas for discipline in schools and talking to fellow teachers are helpful resources for determining solutions.

In contrast, how do non-inquiring teachers solve classroom management and discipline problems? They make no attempt to help students internalize values and rely on external controls, either punishments or rewards. All the decisions and rules come from the top and are enforced by the power adults have over children. In other words, it's "do as I say because I know best." This is reactive discipline rather than classroom community leadership. Teachers respond to the immediate "misbehavior" instead of determining the underlying causes. This style may work in the short term, but teachers who resort to it neglect their responsibility to consider long-term community goals.

Summary

A very specific view or model of discipline and classroom management has been presented in this chapter. Instead of understanding "discipline" as the use of strategies to manipulate behavior to get students to do what you want when you want them to do it, democratic classroom community leaders view discipline as the process of developing and nurturing self-control in the context of democratic community membership. Discipline encourages students of all ages to be autonomous or self-governing. The teacher is the dynamic leader who sets up a democratic society in which norms are established by all the participants. It is a safe, good place to be for adults and young people.

Classroom community leadership is a deliberative process involving the establishment of democratic community norms, the thoughtful analysis and resolution of classroom disruptions to these norms, and the facilitation of student autonomy based on democratic values, all in the context of curriculum leadership. Classroom community leadership is highly inquiring and is guided by a rich set of value considerations.

TEACHER INSIGHTS

Johnny Jackson

I think this model of classroom community leadership is ideal. It makes students self-disciplined and moves them toward the goal of uncovering the natural world order. Becoming familiar with role models who are real examples of the democratic traditions, who are exemplars of leaders, helps students (and even other teachers) see how leadership is possible in the community of the classroom. I am excited about the possibilities. Let me elaborate.

There is a structure to each academic tradition that can help to counteract the disorder prevalent in many children's lives. Through a democratic classroom, students can pursue an order that is necessary in a learning environment. All children need to have a place where they can find the peace and tranquility necessary for learning and thinking.

It is essential that our modern youngsters become grounded in our cultural heritage and begin to use great people and great ideas as their self-disciplinary models. The mental challenge of deep intellectual pursuit immerses students of all ages in the universal activities that constitute our "humanity." This is especially important in a community that practices the ethic of caring and values the humanness of colleagues.

This mental challenge must be developmentally facilitated. Teachers can turn to Piaget for guidance in helping students to construct moral knowledge for themselves. This great epistemologist identified the stages of intellectual and moral growth. He hypothesized that our mental structures grow step-by-step through the complex processes of assimilation and accommodation. Teachers facilitate these processes by providing students with concrete experiences. When we talk about classroom management (even the term *management* sounds too impersonal and mechanistic), we are really talking about how students progressively learn to work with and get along with others. The classroom has to be designed to encourage students to construct their own knowledge about what it takes to live ethically in society. The only way to get to higher levels of both knowledge and moral action is to actively engage in learning and the pursuit of that knowledge. Likewise, to reach higher levels of moral reasoning, students must have opportunities to interact with others in morally more advanced ways.

How do I envision this happening in a classroom? The answer is through a developmentally aware, discipline-based curriculum. Content areas such as literature and social studies offer wonderful opportunities to exercise moral reasoning. A great literary work such as Shakespeare's *Julius Caesar* can stimulate discussion about correct behavior, set behavior goals, and model the purest and best ways to act. The character of Atticus Finch in the novel *To Kill A Mockingbird* can teach a student a lot about respect for other human beings and acting in moral and courageous ways. Adler's *Six Great Ideas* deals directly with the concepts of democracy and justice. Of course, the curriculum has to be set up so that it engages students and allows them to develop cognitively, to expand their horizons, to see other perspectives, and to be cognitively aware. Playing a board game can help students see other points of view and practice critical thinking skills as they interpret and apply rules, develop playing strategies, and so on. Finding and using different means to help students actively confront their moral and intellectual growth is an imaginative challenge for the classroom teacher.

Modeling encourages students' developmental processes. If you problem solve as a teacher in the classroom, encourage the students to do the same. Make it a part of every activity. Teachers have to read and have respect for our traditions. The norms in the classroom have to include love of knowledge and respect for beauty and culture. Some recitation and memorization may be necessary, but problem-solving and thoughtfulness should predominate. Gary Griffin (1989) advocates "expectations for learning that lead to problem solving rather than recall and recitation as disposition and habit" (p. 280). Those expectations must be classroom norms. For example, if students are coming into class late, tell them, "We have a problem here. What can we do about it?" Give them the chance to work with unbounded problems and come up with different solutions. Point out situations in which students can practice problem solving skills with your assistance.

As I stated in the beginning of my discourse, biographies of people like Thomas Jefferson help students appreciate the importance of the democratic tradition, both throughout our history and right now, in our classroom. High school students need to read and discuss biographies of great and famous people, such as Frank Lloyd Wright or Franklin D. Roosevelt. Discuss how they developed their talents, how they affected people, and what kinds of contributions they have made to our society. Help the students construct knowledge not only about the world, but about how they will act in it and upon it.

Practice and hard work seem like out-of-date notions for our almost-21st-century lives, but being committed to gaining important knowledge trains the mind and affects the body.

I'm going to illustrate how I would use the mental checklist introduced in this chapter to implement classroom community leadership. Let's say two students begin to fight in the classroom. I know right away in Step 1 that this behavior violates the norms of the community. I would skip to Step 3, take immediate action to stop it, and remind the students of the expectation that they not hurt anyone in the classroom. Then, going back to Step 2, perhaps I would see that this behavior occurred because these two students were not sufficiently engaged in their assignments and need to learn some self-control. I would give a motivational lecture about the assignment to get them involved, and I would also point out examples of great people who had to gain discipline in order to achieve. Finally, in Step 4, I would have the students read a biography of Franklin D. Roosevelt and write a brief summary of what lessons they could learn from his life.

Susan Smith

I like this model of classroom community leadership because it recognizes the importance of discipline in the classroom. The mental checklist is a good example of how to organize discipline strategies. To be effective, you must plan ahead, anticipate possible dangers, and act before the students are negatively impacted.

I doubt if anyone would dispute the importance of the teacher mastering how to get and maintain classroom order. A lot of research in the last 20 years shows empirically how to best and most effectively manage and organize a classroom. It isn't a mystery. The goal of the classroom should be to have students learn, be on task. We have all seen enough chaotic classrooms to know that learning and democracy require well-ordered environment.

To use a business metaphor, the classroom is a dynamic management system that requires the teacher's full attention. Many factors enter into the complex picture. Certainly the teacher must establish and maintain classroom procedures and rules. Students can have input, but the teacher is responsible for making the rules and the consequences for breaking them explicit. Effective managers set and communicate clear expectations and standards. This furthers democratic values. The norms for our society are presented in a way that students, our future citizens, can understand and follow.

The teacher needs to plan for and anticipate behavior problems just as he or she plans for lessons. Teachers should consider students' abilities, content, grouping, and other factors that affect learning when making the daily schedule.

> Teachers who are successful classroom managers have mastered techniques for planning activities and maintaining high levels of student involvement in those activities, for enriching the classroom environment, for anticipating organizational and behavioral problems, and for monitoring students' progress. (Lemlech, 1990, pp. 77–78)

Experienced teachers know that the first three weeks of the school year are the crucial time for teaching their students how to conform to classroom rules and regulations. As much as possible, students should be taught the classroom community's rules through positive reinforcement. At intermittent times when an individual student, group of students, or the entire class is behaving correctly, the teacher can congratulate them on their good conduct. The teacher should create as positive and trusting environment as possible. Only when rules are broken—and only after clearly stated warnings—should teachers resort to punishments. These punishments should be selected primarily for their instructional value. Remember, the overall goal is to provide community leadership to immature "citizens," not to control wayward students.

For example, if a student is continuously talking out of turn, the teacher might ask a parent to help teach the child a lesson by taking away one half hour of television-viewing time when the child interrupts a family member. The teacher might take away five minutes of recess time when the infraction occurs in school. Once the behavior improves, the punishment is stopped. The child has learned a valuable lesson about human communication—perhaps more valuable than a successfully completed reading or math exercise.

The teacher is responsible for overseeing the socialization of students into the system and being aware of how all the components work together to establish a positive and effective learning environment. The role of the teacher as a dynamic classroom leader really is about being an effective classroom manager. The classroom can be a mini-democracy, but the focus should be on those factors that research has proven effective in promoting students' learning and their ability to make empirically based judgments. Unless students achieve, are literate, and practice self-control, our democracy has no future.

I would like to use the checklist to outline how I would deal with the same problem Johnny talked about—a fight in the classroom between two students. I agree that this behavior violates classroom norms and must be stopped immediately. But I view the cause as something else. These two kids are not on task; if they were, they wouldn't be fighting. The issue is getting them to do their work and clarifying expectations. I would act by walking around the room more often to monitor their work. I might place one of the two students close to my desk. Periodically I would ask the class questions about the work to make sure they understand it well enough to be able to do it independently at home. The consequences for the actions would be calling their parents to tell them that fighting is not tolerated in my room under any circumstances, and that the next violation of that norm would require a face-to-face conference.

My view of the classroom seems most popular, and there are many good books about classroom management. Most books about classroom discipline, especially books about assertive discipline and effective teaching practices, will also help you learn more about the management approach to classroom community leadership.

Dennis Sage

This model of classroom community leadership works because it addresses people's basic need for recognition of their individuality while showing them the importance of mutual respect and care. Although I tend to reject models and checklists, the open-endedness of these allow me to use them in ways that make sense to me and reflect my own personal values.

Let me begin by stating what I think is important. The best life is the contemplative life in which one constantly considers democratic values and how to treat other human beings with respect. I am not surprised that so many students are hyperactive in the classroom. The pace is unbearable. Students have no time to just sit, and think, and be alone. Young people seem like they are so wound up that they are on the verge of breaking apart. You have to calm down, slow down, and tune in to your feelings and others' feelings. Ignoring the contemplative nature of human beings is courting disaster. I just hate the feelings of tension, stress, and anxiety I get when I walk into most classrooms. If you take the time to notice, you can feel it.

In a healthy classroom a flow or an energy moves the teacher and the students to the teachable moment when there is that click of understanding. Everyone has experienced it. When that happens, it makes the job of teaching totally worthwhile. It's what a teacher works for. That's what classroom management is all about—getting to that moment.

How do you get control of kids? Your whole being is there with them. You are present in a real way. There is no pretend acting and you tune into the real kids in front of you. You encourage them to be there for you and for each other, as well. You need to make time for students to think, to be alone, to be concerned and caring for each other. Give them time to simply talk about what's important to them, to encourage sharing with and even love for each other.

A teacher needs a certain kind of wisdom to know about children and young adults, to know about content, and to capture all the elements that create a positive environment conducive to learning. When students come to trust the adult in the classroom, they no longer have to act out to get attention. They get into the flow, the rhythm of the group.

The school itself presents the greatest obstructions to establishing a positive learning community. So much time and energy are lost for paperwork and frequent interruptions—time and energy a teacher desperately needs to establish relationships with young people, and with other adults in the building as well. We have to look at teaching and discipline holistically. Van Manen (1991) notes that the term *discipline* comes from the word *disciple,* which means someone who follows a great teacher. A teacher must be able to inspire his or her students. Through sensitive, caring interactions the teacher models what it is like to be a member of a trusting social community. When students feel a desire to be like their teacher, whom they see as kind and concerned about others, then the teacher has succeeded in establishing a positive leadership presence. Then the students are learning appropriate conduct in the most concrete way—through positive adult example.

As a professional you need to develop your most nurturing, loving skills in order to have significant impact on students of every age. You have to be thoughtful, caring, and in touch with yourself through meditation, support groups, or perhaps through a relationship with nature. Find these qualities of empathy, sympathy, kindness, patience and love of young people and continue to develop them. This can only happen in a free, open classroom in which students and teacher make important decisions together democratically.

Using the same example of a classroom disruption, I would like to explain how I would handle the situation. If two students were fighting in class, I would, of course, consider this a violation of classroom norms and stop it immediately. But I might determine that the cause for this altercation is the frenzied pace of the school day and the tremendous pressure children feel to produce. That would lead me to give the students meditation breaks to collect their thoughts and reduce their anxiety levels. Maybe I would have students gather in small support groups to talk to each other about their problems and concerns. I would see this not as taking time away from their studies, but rather as enhancing them. Finally, I would remind students of their ongoing responsibility to be the very best people they can be.

Sylvia Rivera

Although, I generally find these kinds of models to be naive, I like the model of classroom community leadership because it recognizes and respects the fact that schools and classrooms don't exist in a vacuum. Rather they are set in complex contexts where easy solutions to complicated problems don't exist.

Problems in the classroom are tied to problems outside in the community. Unfairness and injustice are rampant in our world. Just using external control to get kids to blindly follow authority doesn't work in the long run. Look at totalitarian governments. You can't control people forever. That goes for school as well as society. As Alfie

Kohn says, "There aren't enough M & M's to keep people on track, to manipulate behavior once they leave the high-surveillance school setting" (1990, p. 53).

The aim of education is to encourage students to be proactive, to change society, to make a difference. They need to know about discrimination in terms of class, race, socioeconomic status, and religion. Rather than regard schooling merely as preparation for living in the existing social order, we should regard it as preparation for taking action to improve the social order. Wood (1988) notes that "primary to any sense of democratic life is the notion that individuals are free to remake the social order in ways that best suit collective needs" (p. 166). In other words, we live in a fluid society; how and what changes are made are determined by its citizens. The task before the school is to empower these future citizens, these future change-makers. That is another reason why I think this leadership model based on a democratic society is right on target.

The curriculum, what we teach and how we teach it, is laden with values. Did you ever think about who decides what's important to teach? There is no list of right things to teach. Decisions about the curriculum are made by teachers, and we teachers must constantly consider how we can make the classroom promote democracy.

One way is to have students become empowered decision-makers in the classroom. Wood (1988) says, "when individuals participate in decisions that directly affect them, they both develop the confidence that such action is possible as well as the desire to participate in even broader public debates" (p. 180). What kinds of decisions can students make? Choosing reading materials, room decorations, or room management are a few examples. Right now certain views of discipline prohibit students from becoming empowered decision-makers. For example, in behavior modification the teacher stipulates rules and punishments and the students follow blindly.

The notion of lifelong learning has to become part of the teacher's and the students' world view. The walls of the school classroom vanish as we see that education is a part of daily living. I never let school get in the way of education. We have to constantly be aware that academic goals, for example, learning to read and write, also help students participate in the larger society, both during their school years and after they leave.

The classroom needs to offer students both personal power and the skills necessary to participate in a collaborative and cooperative environment. In a real way students of all ages can take responsibility for doing relevant, useful work and for deciding on consequences for not doing it. Students can investigate books in all content areas to check for racist, classist, and sexist language. Contemporary social problems provide a wealth of opportunities for discussion and problem solving. Students can address injustice and inequity within the school and work on projects that involve the greater good of society as a whole. All this encourages students to become and remain dedicated opponents of injustice and inequity.

I would like to comment on how I would respond to the problem of two students fighting in the classroom. I have to agree with my colleagues in recognizing this as a problem and stopping it before someone gets hurt. But I believe the cause of the problem lies elsewhere. The lives of these two students are probably very unrelated to the classroom. The way they solve problems in their own lives is probably closer to fighting than to the norms of the classroom community. People respond in ways that are familiar, not necessarily in ways that are the most reasonable. I would have the class meet as a decision-making body to deal directly with the problem of fighting in the classroom. What would they suggest be done? I would let them determine the consequences. Then I would feel responsible for setting up an environment that is safe enough for these young people to take intellectual, emotional and physical chances. I would reconsider how I could provide a safe haven for students so they could really internalize these norms and work on self-discipline.

Personal-Professional Inquiry

1. Describe your past positive experiences with discipline. What do you remember as being positive about these experiences?
2. Describe your past negative experiences with discipline. What was negative about these experiences?
3. Have you experienced a parent, relative, teacher or some other significant adult as a positive role model for discipline? If so, why was this person a positive role model?
4. Have you experienced a negative role model in terms of discipline? If so, why was this person a negative role model?
5. Using the term "classroom community leader" as your nucleus, create a cluster.
6. What problems do you anticipate during student teaching that center around classroom community leadership? How would these be different if they were treated as classroom management issues?

7. Make a list of the norms you think are important for your classroom community. Make a list of norms you think are important for the school community.
8. How do you show your best self through classroom community leadership? How do you bring out your students' best selves through classroom community leadership?
9. How do you plan to find a mentor who can help you develop as a caring classroom community leader? Who can that person be and what role can he or she play in your professional development?
10. Which teacher character's advice do you find most compatible with your point of view? Do you find that each teacher character has insights into classroom community leadership that appeal to you?

Further Readings

In addition to the materials recommended by each of the teacher-characters, the following sources will help you learn more about classroom community leadership.

ADLER, M. (1982). *The paideia proposal: An educational manifesto.* New York: Macmillan.

CANFIELD, J., & WELLS, H. C. (1976). *100 ways to enhance the classroom.* Englewood, NJ: Prentice-Hall.

CHARLES, C. M. (1985). *Building classroom discipline: From models to practice.* New York: Longman.

CLARIZO, H. F. (1971). *Toward positive classroom discipline.* New York: Wiley & Sons.

CURWIN, R., & MENDLERS, A. (1989). *Discipline with dignity.* Alexandria, VA: Association of Supervision and Curriculum Development.

DEWEY, J. (1902). *The child and the curriculum.* Chicago: University of Chicago Press.

DEWEY, J. (1927). *The public and its problems.* New York: Henry Holt.

EMMER, E. T., EVERSTON, C. M., SANFORD, J. P., CLEMENTS, B. S., & WORSHAM, M. E. (1989). *Classroom management for secondary teachers* (2nd ed.). Englewood Cliffs, NJ: Prentice-Hall.

EVERTSON, C. M., EMMER, E. T., CLEMENTS, B. S., SANFORD, J. P., & WORSHAM, M. E. (1984). *Classroom management for elementary teachers.* Englewood Cliffs, NJ: Prentice-Hall.

GLASSER, W. (1975). *Schools without failure.* New York: Harper & Row.

GLASSER, W. (1985). *Control theory in the classroom.* New York: Harper & Row.

GREENE, M. (1988). *The dialectic of freedom.* New York: Teachers College Press.

JIRSILD, A. T. (1955). *When teachers face themselves.* New York: Teachers College Press.

KOHLBERG, L. (1980). High school democracy and education for a just society. In R. L. Mosher (Ed.), *Moral education* (pp. 20–57). New York: Praeger.

PUBLIC EDUCATION INFORMATION NETWORK. (1985). *Education for a democratic future.* St. Louis, MO: Author.

RAYWID, M. A., TESCONI, C. A., and WARREN, D. R. (1984). *Pride and promise: Schools of excellence for all people.* Westbury, NY: American Educational Studies Association.

ROGERS, C. R. (1983). *Freedom to learn for the 80's.* Columbus, OH: Merrill.

SARASON, S. B. (1982). *The culture of the school and the problem of change* (2nd. ed.). Boston: Allyn & Bacon.

SHOR, I. (1987). *Critical teaching and everyday life.* Chicago: University of Chicago Press.

References

ADLER, M. (1981). *Six great ideas.* NY: Macmillan.

BANDURA, A., and WALTERS, R. H. (1963). *Social learning and personality development.* NY: Holt, Rinehart and Winston.

DREIKURS, R. (1982). *Maintaining sanity in the classroom* (2nd ed.). NY: Harper & Row.

ENCYCLOPAEDIA BRITANNICA CORPORATION. (1990). *Rethinking urban schools: The Chicago agenda.* Chicago: Author.

FLORIO-RUANE, S. (1989). Social organization of classes and schools. In M. C. Reynolds (Ed.), *Knowledge base for the beginning teacher* (pp. 163–172). Oxford: Pergamon Press.

GRIFFIN, G. (1989). Coda: The knowledge-driven school. In M. C. Reynolds (Ed.), *Knowledge base for the beginning teacher* (pp. 277–286). Oxford: Pergamon Press.

KOHN, A. (1990). The abc's of caring. *Teacher, 1*(4), 52–58.

LEMLECH, J. K. (1990). *Curriculum and instructional methods for the elementary school* (2nd ed.). NY: Macmillan.

LORTIE, D. C. (1975). *School teacher.* Chicago: University of Chicago Press.

PIAGET, J. (1973). *The moral judgment of the child* (M. Gabain, Trans.). New York: Free Press. (Original work published 1932)

SCHAPS, E., & SOLOMON, D. (1990). Schools and classrooms as caring communities. *Educational Leadership, 48*(3), 38–42.

VAN MANEN, M. (1991). *The tact of teaching: The meaning of pedagogical thoughtfulness.* Albany, NY: State University of New York Press.

WAYSON, W. W. (1984). Opening windows to teaching: Empowering educators to teach self-discipline. *Theory Into Practice, 24*(4), 227–232.

WOOD, G. H. (1988). Democracy and education. In L. E. Beyer & M. W. Apple (Eds.), *The curriculum: Problems, politics, and possibilities* (pp. 166–185). NY: State University of New York Press.

WOOD, G. H. (1990). Teaching for democracy. *Educational Leadership 48*(3), 32–37.

CHAPTER 7

Collaborative Inquiry

Introduction

Teachers have difficulty engaging in reflective teaching and educational inquiry if they feel isolated in their own classrooms (Darling-Hammond, 1988; Lieberman, 1988; Lortie, 1975). Reflective teaching and educational inquiry are challenging undertakings, and you may find this challenge much easier to accept if you receive some collegial assistance. In this chapter you will be introduced to two collaborative inquiry activities. They are called *collegial professional development* and *peer coaching*, and they are both based on the concept of cooperative learning.

Prerequisites to Collaborative Inquiry

Cooperative learning has become a major movement in education. One of the leaders of this movement, Robert Slavin, observed that the "Age of Cooperation is approaching. From Alaska to California to Florida to New York, from Australia to Britain to Norway to Israel, teachers and administrators are discovering an untapped resource for accelerating students' achievement: the students themselves" (Slavin, 1987, p. 7). You will find that the cooperative learning experiences in this chapter will further your personal growth as you develop your values, goals, and skills as a student of teaching. Later, in your own classroom, you are likely to confirm that cooperative learning activities are among the most successful, enjoyable, and rewarding experiences you can offer your students.

The concept of cooperative learning covers a diverse assortment of activities ranging from group playwriting to partner test-taking. No matter what the activity, students must possess certain social skills to participate effectively. Slavin (1990) describes the importance of prerequisite social skills such as interpersonal communication, conflict management, and group interaction. If you attended typical elementary and secondary schools that emphasized individual competition, you may need to work on your cooperative learning skills before engaging in the collaborative learning activities in this chapter. Johnson (1981) has identified a list of the social skills associated with collaborative inquiry activities. Though there is no one-to-one correspondence between these skills and the chapter's activities, you may find the list to be a helpful diagnostic tool. Recommendations for the further study of topics on this list are included at the end of this chapter.

- Self disclosing
- Developing and maintaining trust
- Communicating with others
- Listening and responding
- Accepting yourself and others
- Resolving interpersonal conflicts
- Confronting and negotiating
- Managing anger and stress

Collegial Professional Development: An Overview

Collegial professional development is a cooperative activity with two main purposes. A small group of approximately six teaching "colleagues" meets as a support group to discuss their personal interpretations of good teaching. Members of the group respect each other's points of view because they are bound by an ethic of caring, with its reference to each individual's best teaching self, and because they all believe in the enduring value of constructivist learning.

However, collegial professional development is not an unconditionally supportive activity. Constructive criticism is accepted and encouraged. As members of the group share their individual professional understandings, they open themselves to public scrutiny. They know that their interpretations of good teaching can be examined. Do their ideas make sense to their peers? Are they overly idealistic? Are they sincerely inquiring into their sense of professionalism? These types of questions are openly explored during a collegial professional development activity.

Collegial professional development groups can choose from a diverse assortment of discussion topics. Groups should employ two criteria to make the selection: personal relevance and comfort level. All group members should agree that a chosen topic is worthwhile; discussing a meaningless topic on good teaching is a charade that violates the very spirit of constructivist learning. Just as importantly, members of the group must feel able to be both supportive *and* critical on a particular teaching topic. If this is not the case, that topic should be avoided.

You will now be introduced to two forms of collegial professional development, inquiry dialogue and further readings dialogue. Keep the general description of collegial professional development in mind as you study these activities.

Inquiry Dialogue

Your personal-professional inquiries in chapters 4 through 6 can serve as the topic for a collegial professional development group. How did each person respond to the questions at the end of the chapters? Did anyone answer additional questions? Did anyone reject some of the questions as irrelevant or too personal? What do educational problem solving, curriculum leadership and classroom community leadership mean to each member of the group? What are each member's professional values for these three topics?

To help you prepare for this collaborative inquiry experience, your group may first want to read and discuss the following essay written by a preservice student in response to the inquiries in chapters 4 through 6.

✷ As I completed the personal-professional inquiries at the end of each chapter, several things about myself began to emerge. I began to see the limitations that suburban life had placed on my perceptions, and I started to identify the educational issues I felt strongly about. These were things I had inside of me but wouldn't have realized without exploring myself through inquiry and being exposed to the perceptions of my peers whose life experiences differed from my own. By being allowed to freely inquire into these areas, I was able to identify and further establish my own standards about education and the action I needed to take to move towards these ideal standards. I realize, of course, that I may not have the freedom of such personalized opportunities after I have entered the profession; there may be administrators and department heads who will not agree with my standards and who may pressure me with standardized evaluations to conform to their ideals. However, there are others who feel and think as I do—that teacher autonomy and caring are important in education.

Part of my professional development as a student will be to establish a support group consisting of other students, administrators, and teachers who share my perspective on education and can work together towards these ideals through sharing ideas, encouragement, and empathy. The one thing I always try to remember is that, in anything I do, I have the right to pursue it according to my own standards, while still recognizing that I must adapt my standards to the situation. Sometimes my pursuit of personal excellence may have to be subtle because of a top-down situation, but my pursuit is never surrendered.

In general, I have found that the development of personal standards takes courage, commitment, and a great deal of critical thinking, but the resulting self-confidence and determination are worth the struggle. As you write the inquiry essays, you find yourself questioning your conceptualizations of "right" and "wrong." Instead of clear-cut answers, you begin to recognize that there are degrees to what, and when, you see something as acceptable or even desirable. For example, having students record their own family trees in a community with predominantly single parent families may generate student anxiety or resentment, but in another community the activity may generate enthusiasm because it stimulates family involvement. The field of education is a complex one.

The reflective thought for the inquiries is also a tool to identify when you're locked into a specific view, thereby preventing you from examining other dimensions which should be considered. The self-questioning vital to the inquiries is a way to continually improve your personal standards and professional growth. Differences of opinion result in reflection. Have I fully considered that view? Am I rejecting it because it is different from what I've always considered to be "right"? Are both views justifiable? During conversation with peers, it becomes clear that there are no "right" standards—only justifiable ones. Once a group has accepted this reality, a level of tolerance for new ideas develops among peers who share in mutual respect. From this environment springs the support of encouragement, constructive criticism, and shared ideas.

Do you respect this student's point of view? Do you feel you could be both supportive and constructively critical of her ideas? Why, or why not? As your group discusses these (and perhaps related) questions, you will begin to discover one another's personal and professional values. You will then be in a better position to decide whether you are comfortable collaborating over your own inquiries.

Further Readings Dialogue

Chapters 4 through 6 ended with a Further Readings section that can serve as the topical focus for your collaborative group. Each group member designs a personally relevant professional development project, and determines a project time line. The time line establishes a schedule for periodic progress reports, the final presentation, and a group critique of the project.

Projects should be guided by the following four questions:

1. Based on my educational problem solving, curriculum leadership, and/or classroom community leadership inquiries, what are my professional development needs?
2. How do these needs relate to my emerging professional values?
3. What specific activities can I undertake to meet my professional development needs?
4. As I engage in these activities, how will I know I am making progress in meeting my needs?

The following professional development projects were designed respectively by a preservice elementary education student and a secondary education student. The elementary education student's project was designed on a 3-week time line as part of a field-experience course, while the secondary education student's project was designed on a 6-week time line in a university-based seminar.

✱ *The Elementary Education Project*

My Professional Development Needs

1. *For educational problem solving.* I need to be able to handle problems when they occur in the classroom and not relegate them until a later time or, worse yet, relegate them to others. I need to be more confident in my ability to solve problems on my own, as well, but I need to keep in mind when it would be best to enlist the help of others in solving these problems.
2. *For curriculum leadership.* I need to work on promoting positive learning transactions in the classroom. I need to especially utilize task analysis with ease in every subject I teach.
3. *For classroom curriculum leadership.* I need to learn how to effectively create classroom community norms that, while not overly rigid in structure, are stringent enough to maintain discipline in the classroom. I need to work on learning to effectively implement reality therapy techniques in my classroom.

My Professional Values

1. *For educational problem solving.* As an active problem solver I should be a critical and analytical thinker. I should try to see all the parts of any problem I encounter and delve deeply in order to solve it. I should be aware of both current and potential problems in the classroom. I should handle both bounded and unbounded problems to the best of my ability. I should also be objective, caring, and understanding in my problem solving methods.
2. *For curriculum leadership.* As a curriculum leader I should be motivated as well as motivating. I should have clear, concise lesson plans that are grade-level appropriate. I should also try to always take into account my students' needs, both past and present, when teaching my lessons.
3. *For classroom community leadership.* As a classroom community leader I should set a good example for the students in the area of discipline through my behavior in the classroom and by handling discipline problems to the best of my ability at this time. I should see discipline problems as problems of poor internalization of classroom norms and try to make sure that all classroom norms are clearly stated to the students. I believe that violations of classroom community norms are best handled through the use of strategies of internalization (e.g. reality therapy).

Activities

Over a 3-week period (for approximately 5 hours per week), I will conduct individual conferences with students in an elementary-grade classroom. Our topic will be current problems and potential problems they foresee. These individual student conferences will be organized to practice active problem solving. We will first talk about what the problem is. I will then suggest ways to solve the problem and encourage the student to think about ways to solve the problem. Once we have come up with some ideas, we'll talk about just how we'll go about solving the problem. Finally, we'll discuss follow-up strategies to make sure the problem is getting solved. I will keep a journal of all of these student conferences. I may also try an entire classroom problem-solving session based on the same approach. We would discuss a common classroom problem and then go through the problem-solving procedures.

Evidence of Accomplishment

I will collect two types of evidence to determine if I am becoming a better problem solver in the classroom. I will ask other people at the school, such as an experienced teacher, to observe some of my practice teaching. I'll ask them to tell me if I'm getting better at handling problems before they escalate. I want to know if I am acting quickly and not ignoring problems. The journal notes I'll be taking for the individual conferences (and perhaps the large classroom conference) could be studied to see if I'm getting better at following the problem solving procedure I've set up.

The Secondary Education Project

My Professional Development Needs

My professional needs reflect what other people have said about me, including parents, brother, and supervisors. I have a tendency to become complacent, which is probably fallout from my laidback persona. I need to remind myself to keep applying the important aspects of problem solving. I have also found that I sometimes confront problems in a hostile manner. For some reason, my initial reaction to a problem is often defensive. I need to shift my approach to a more positive perspective. I also tend towards a shallow perspective on problems. My personal habits and routines limit my responses to problems. I need to recognize what my limiting factors are and to work around them. I am quite reluctant to show personal caring—perhaps it is part of my defensive nature—but I need to learn how to do so.

Most of my needs regarding curriculum leadership center around my lack of experience in a leadership role. An aspect of my personality is that I feel more comfortable when I overplan lessons. I need to allow some flexibility. I know that today's students are different from those of 20 years ago. I need to find out what motivates them. Today's students have so many forces fighting for their attention. School is simply not as strong a part of their lives as it might have been in the past. Until now, I have been more a follower in life. I need to adopt measures which will make it clear that I am now the leader. A final central need which I must address is that of actively reflecting upon what is occurring during a lesson and adapting my teaching according to the conditions. To be a leader, I must become more flexible.

I need to reflect on the classroom behavior I want to uphold. If I go into a classroom without a clear concept of this behavior, I cannot guide others. Of course, these reflections will consider community values as well. I need to know what norms are expected from today's students in most classrooms. I need to know how to deal with students who have different socioeconomic backgrounds than mine. Most teachers will have students from families with different backgrounds. I need to be able to deal with them. Presently, I do not know how I would deal with students with different backgrounds.

My Professional Values

Initiating a professional development project is a soul-searching experience. The very nature of such an experience means that it is binding in terms of fulfilling the objectives. It also means that along the way, as your experiences are examined, your project can be amended and expanded as you deem necessary.

My initial thoughts on educational problem solving were that as time went on, I would build a storehouse of solutions for all the problems I will face as a teacher. It is very reassuring to think that way. The only problem is that you can never be sure you are pulling the correct solution, or the best one, from your collection. As an active problem solver, I want to continually be aware that predicaments will always exist, and I should be seeking them out. Once I recognize them, I will strive for the best solution. No problem will be dismissed.

My standards for curriculum leadership center around the student. The class and lessons are for them and no one else. Every facet of planning and reviewing lessons should be justifiable in regards to student development. I want to motivate students and to be flexible. Lesson plans, no matter the effort put into them, should never be engraved in stone. I think a teacher should lead by example. My actions will speak volumes about who I am, and students will react accordingly. I will always be "on stage" with students. I am the leader. While I believe students are partners in the learning process, the teacher is the authority who governs that relationship. To be effective, I need control over myself, the class, and the topic. I know that even a leader needs help. Few are so far developed that no one can help. As an instructional leader, I realize the importance of having a rapport with my peers. Collaborative discussions should be the release valve for anyone who begins to think they are in this alone.

The classroom community leader will demonstrate and adhere to the norms of the larger society, and it should be a priority of mine to know the norms of the community in which I teach. While parents are the primary influence for many children, teachers may be the only positive role model for many others. There are no promises that I will "save" any students from a poorer quality of life, but I certainly must try. I will try to enculturate my students to my utmost ability. In the process, I realize that there are no absolutes. Norms are somewhat relative depending upon the background of the student. I want to get the students on my side and then work with them. Throughout my career, I want to be involved and concerned with my positive impact on others, including my peers. We are not alone. We are part of a teaching community, and our colleagues need our support.

Activities

To become more aware of how I deal with problems, I will log problem incidents I am experiencing and the way I am dealing with them. Since I also want to confront problems in a more creative and understanding manner, I will read *The IDEAL Problem Solver* (Bransford & Stein, 1984) and write a summary of that approach. I plan to develop a solution-strategy mind-set for problems I think will be common for beginning teachers. While I do not believe in having ready-to use solutions, having a philosophy of educational problem solving will get me prepared. I will interview a teacher acknowledged as excellent in classroom management. A written summary of her approach will serve as a helpful guide. Finally, I want to become more caring. I plan to read a book by Buscaglia (1982), *Living, Loving and Learning*, to reaffirm this goal.

In order to introduce more spontaneity into my lessons, I plan to write several lesson plans which have points of flexibility built in. I plan to read and summarize several recent articles on what motivational techniques are being used successfully. I will define what leadership skills I need in the classroom. To help me with this activity, I will read and summarize *Discovering Your Teaching Self* (Curwin & Fuhrmann, 1975).

To address my needs, I must begin by finding out my norms. I will describe my personal set of norms that can apply to any classroom student, and I will have the justifications for each. I will interview several teachers and list the norms they believe in. Part of being a leader is maintaining students' behavior. I will read *Assertive Discipline* (Canter & Canter, 1976) and summarize how I might apply the ideas in this book to my own caring teaching and community leadership.

I plan to complete all these activities in a 6-week period.

Evidence of Accomplishment

My log book, my *The IDEAL Problem Solver* (Bransford, 1984) summary, and my interview summary should all indicate that I am working on meeting my needs.

My lesson plans should demonstrate points of flexibility. My article summaries will show I have studied new motivational techniques. My summary of *Discovering Your Teaching Self* (Curwin & Fuhrmann 1975), and my skills list will show that I'm getting clearer on my leadership skills.

My two lists of norms will show I'm working on my community leadership, and my summary of *Assertive Discipline* (Canter & Canter, 1976) will demonstrate I'm thinking about ways to help my students follow the norms I will establish.

Peer Coaching

The second type of collaborative inquiry activity in this chapter is called *peer coaching*. Peer coaching affords teachers the opportunity to provide feedback on one another's teaching. Think of a peer coaching team as a self-help community. There are many types of peer coaching, and a complete description of all the possibilities for this type of professional collaboration would require an entire book.

Like collegial professional development, peer coaching serves the two goals of peer support and constructive criticism. Joyce and Showers (1983) describe the first goal as follows: "The coaching relationship results in the possibility of mutual reflection, the checking of perceptions, the sharing of frustrations and successes, and the informal thinking through of mutual problems" (p. 19). When you are part of a good coaching team, you are a member of a professional support group that encourages you to be openly exploratory and inquiring.

The dialogue among members of a good peer coaching team is constructively critical at times. Good coaches are honest about their peer's teaching. If they feel some aspect of their colleague's instruction needs improvement, they will offer their genuine assessment. They know that, in the spirit of collegiality, this feedback doesn't have to be accepted, but at least it has been offered. Furthermore, they hope their honesty will be reciprocated.

You will now explore two forms of peer coaching, group peer coaching and partner peer coaching. Keep the general description of peer coaching in mind as you study these two examples.

Group Peer Coaching

A group peer coaching activity has three phases: planning, implementation, and feedback. During the planning phase team members discuss the specifics of their collegial interaction. Will each member select an individual teaching topic, or will a common topic be determined? The choices of relevant teaching topics are unlimited. Your individual constructivist work in chapters 4 through 6 may suggest a particular topic. For example, discussion could focus on solving a specific classroom learning problem; teaching a lesson or part of a lesson; or analyzing a disciplinary activity. The team will need to decide on the duration of the selected teaching topic and on who will be the "students" for the collaborative activity. Will the members of the team role play a certain grade level of students, or will the peer coaching occur in an actual classroom with real students? If the teaching takes place in an actual classroom, should the teacher's peers be present, or would their presence be disruptive? Perhaps the teaching should be videotaped and the coaching feedback based on the tape.

Once the team has made its plans, the implementation phase begins. The quality of the coaches' observations determines the quality of their feedback. The student teacher may ask the coaches to focus on a particular aspect of teaching, such as lesson explanations. The peer coaches may also make their own spontaneous observations of things that need to be brought to their colleague's attention.

When the teaching is completed, the feedback phase of the activity begins. Each peer coach offers both supportive feedback and constructive criticism. Once this collegial sharing has ended, all the team members can engage in another type of feedback. They can critique the quality of their collaborative efforts. How well did they plan? Were their observations helpful, and were the criticisms constructive? How could the group do better next time?

A Description of a Group Peer Coaching Activity

An elementary education student who completed a group peer coaching activity described her experience as follows:

> We formed as a group of six elementary education majors, and we decided that each of us would teach for 20 minutes while the rest of us were the students. Each teacher would then receive 10 minutes of peer coaching. Initially I was nervous about getting up and teaching in front of my group. After about 5 minutes, though, I forgot they were my friends and saw them as my students. I got in the mind-set of being a teacher and having to get my ideas across to my students. Group peer coaching is so much like teaching in real life, except you are only working with about five students. In all other ways, it is the same. I had to plan a lesson, understand the material to be covered, and motivate my group. The most important thing for me was that my peers got into and out of their student roles easily. I didn't have to tell them how to be little again; and when the lesson was over, they instantly reverted back.
>
> As a group, we decided that in every lesson there would be three main areas to cover. First, there had to be an introduction. In this area I told my group what they were expected to do, what grade they were supposed to be, what knowledge of the material they already had, and what subject the lesson was in. The second area to cover was the lesson. I taught my lesson trying to accomplish the objectives I had set as the teacher. When my lesson was over, the third part of our group activity began. This was the feedback. My peers told me what they liked about my lesson, what they thought was especially effective, and what things I could do to improve.
>
> What I learned most from this collegial activity was that teaching is about being interesting. You have to be someone who can motivate a student to want to learn. After we all had taught our lessons, there wasn't any more anxiety. In fact, all of us wanted to continue the group activity. I reflected back after it was all over and realized that everyone had really done a good job. We all had worked together, supported one another, and given good feedback. Each of us got a taste of what teaching would be: the frustration of not getting a point across, the challenge of dealing with a misbehaving student, and the possibility of an unsuccessful lesson. But we also got to see the joy a smile can bring, the fun we can have, and the positive effect we can have as a teacher.

Partner Peer Coaching

Partner peer coaching is very similar to group peer coaching. Partners plan together, observe one another's teaching, and give each other feedback. Pairs may need to share their plans with other members of a collaborative team if the teaching occurs under simulated conditions involving a group of peers.

A Description of a Partner Peer Coaching Activity

The same elementary education student who completed the group peer coaching activity describes her experience with partner peer coaching.

✻ When we finished group peer coaching and went on to partner peer coaching, we all learned a lot more. We each taught for 20 minutes with our partner sitting outside the group, observing our teaching. Everyone else on our elementary education team acted as students. After the teaching, we received 10 minutes of feedback from our partner. Everybody taught first; then we sat down with our partner to share our observations.

I feel that in our group peer coaching activity we were too supportive of one another. We weren't as critical as we could have been, and we tended to see more of the good than, probably, was really there. My peer coaching partner knew ahead of time what my lesson plan was going to be and the areas I wanted her to focus on. She also knew that I wanted her to identify what she thought my weaknesses were. As a result, the teaching feedback I received was very effective and more honest. I got the opinion of one person—someone who spent 20 minutes observing my every word and action. My partner wrote down all of her comments, which I thought was very helpful. I can keep these written notes to review my strengths and see the areas I need to improve. They can serve as my checklist to evaluate whether I'm becoming lax or if I'm actually excelling.

When our group finished the partner peer coaching activity, we talked about our experiences. We all felt really good about ourselves. Before we all had had doubts about whether we were really cut out to be teachers or not. Our partners' words of encouragement and alternative ideas helped a lot, and we experienced a lot of unity. None of us expected more than a partner could give, but we were critical, too. We didn't just accept everything. Because we all kept an open mind-set, we learned something from each lesson—even when we weren't the peer observer.

Overall, we felt we had made great progress. We saw how we had worked together, how much it helps to have other people's advice, and how one idea can be expressed in so many different ways.

Summary

The activities in this chapter have the common goal of encouraging continuous professional development. Good teaching is the result of an ongoing critical study of one's practices, and this chapter has introduced you to four ways to collaborate with others on the study of teaching. Teacher cooperation is certainly not limited to collegial professional development and peer coaching. The potential for peer cooperation is, ultimately, limited only by the commitment and imagination of those involved.

Further Readings

You may want to inquire further into the social skills associated with the collaborative activities in this chapter. The following books will get you started. They are divided into three categories: *Understanding Oneself, Communicating with Others,* and *Sharing Professional Thoughts and Feelings.* At this point in the text, you are undoubtedly aware of the important relationship between self-reflection and collaborative reflection. If your sense of self—or what is sometimes called self-esteem and personal efficacy in education—is underdeveloped, you have a much more difficult time authentically sharing with others. The books listed in all three categories, though they have a slightly different emphasis, sensitively treat this important interpersonal principle.

Understanding Oneself

FRICK, W. B. (1984). *Personality theories: Journeys into self: An experiential workbook.* New York: Teachers College Press.

HOUSTON, J. (1982). *The possible human: A course in enhancing your physical, mental, and creative abilities.* Los Angeles: J. P. Tarcher.

JERSILD, A. T. (1955). *When teachers face themselves.* New York: Teachers College Press.

PEARSON, C. S. (1989). *The hero within.* New York: Harper & Row.

ROGERS, C. (1961). *On becoming a person.* Boston: Houghton Mifflin.

Communicating with Others

EGAN, G. (1975). *The skilled helper.* Monterey, CA: Brooks/Cole.

HARRIS, T. A. (1969). *I'm OK–you're OK: A practical guide to transactional analysis.* New York: Harper & Row.

SMITH, M. J. (1975). *When I say no, I feel guilty.* New York: Bantam Books.

Sharing Professional Thoughts and Feelings

BRANDT, R. S. (Ed.). (1987). Staff development through coaching. [Special issue]. *Educational Leadership, 44*(5).

CONNELLY, M. F., & CLANDININ, D. J. (1988). *Teachers as curriculum planners: Narratives of experience.* New York: Teachers College Press.

Cunard, R. F. (1990). Sharing instructional leadership: A view to strengthening the principal's position. *NASSP Bulletin, 74*(525), 30–34.

Hillkirk, H., Tome, J., & Wandress, W. (1989). Integrating reflection in staff development programs. *Journal of Staff Development, 10*(2), 54–58.

Holly, M. L. (1989). *Writing to grow: Keeping a personal-professional journal.* Portsmouth, NH: Heinemann.

Miller, J. L. (1990). *Creating spaces and finding voices: Teachers collaborating for empowerment.* Albany: State University of New York Press.

Raney, P., & Robbins, P.(1989). Professional growth and support through peer coaching. *Educational Leadership, 47*(8), 35–38.

References

Bransford, J. D., & Stein, B. S. (1984). *The IDEAL problem solver: A guide for improving thinking, learning, and creativity.* New York: Freeman.

Buscaglia, L. F. (1982) *Living, loving and learning.* Thorofare, NJ: Charles B. Slack.

Canter, L., & Canter, M. (1976). *Assertive discipline: A take charge approach for today's educator.* Seal Beach, CA: Canter and Associates.

Curwin, R. L., & Fuhrmann, B. S. (1975). *Discovering your teaching self; humanistic approaches to effective teaching.* Englewood Cliffs, NJ: Prentice-Hall, 1975.

Darling-Hammond, L. (1988). Accountability and teacher professionalism. *American Educator, 12*(4), 8–13, 38–43.

Johnson, D. W. (1981). *Reaching out: Interpersonal effectiveness and self-actualization* (2nd ed.). Englewood Cliffs, NJ: Prentice-Hall.

Joyce, B. R., & Showers, B. (1983). *Power in staff development through research on training.* Alexandria, VA: Association for Supervision and Curriculum Development.

Lieberman, A. (1988). Teachers and principals: Turf, tension, and new tasks. *Phi Delta Kappan, 69*(9), 648–653.

Lortie, D. C. (1975). *Schoolteacher: A sociological study.* Chicago: University of Chicago Press.

Slavin, R. E. (1987). Cooperative learning and the cooperative school. *Educational Leadership, 45*(3), 7–13.

Slavin, R. E. (1990). *Cooperative learning: Theory, research, and practice.* Englewood Cliffs, NJ: Prentice Hall.

CHAPTER 8

Reflecting on Student Learning Problems

Introduction

You now have had the opportunity to experience what it means to be a reflective teacher and an inquiring educator. You have practiced the model of reflective teaching on yourself by considering your own past experiences and personal purposes with reference to educational problem solving, curriculum leadership, and classroom community leadership. You have been encouraged to be inquiring while engaging in this reflection; you've been asked to respond individually and collaboratively to a variety of open-ended questions on various topics. Now you will have the opportunity to practice functioning as a reflective teacher and an inquiring educator on complex cases of student learning problems.

Metacognitive Practice Or Scaffolded Instruction

The design of this chapter is guided by a particular learning principle called *metacognition.* Metacognition is the conscious monitoring of one's thought processes (Haller, Child, & Walberg, 1988; Wittrock, 1986). Think of metacognition as a mental prompt analogous to a prewritten shopping list that you use when you go to the store. You don't mechanically follow this list, but you use it to remind yourself of things you may need. A metacognitive strategy reminds you to consider different types of information and a variety of possible solutions during your problem-solving efforts. The more you begin to regulate your thinking by following conscious mental strategies, particularly in a supportive collegial environment, the better you will be able to integrate these strategies into your everyday conscious and intuitive teaching (Vygotsky, 1978).

Metacognitive practice is sometimes called scaffolded self-instruction. A scaffold is an "adjustable and temporary" support system (Palincsar, 1986, p. 75). In effect, this chapter is providing you with a scaffold to use when reflecting on student learning problems. Use it in this spirit. As you begin to internalize this structured guidance, as you learn to adapt these questions to your own problem-solving style, discard the scaffolding.

In the future you may want to use the principle of metacognition or scaffolded instruction in your teaching. You would provide your students with a conscious structure to monitor their own thinking (during the acts of reading, writing, speaking, computing, and so on) and then help them practice this structure as an adjustable and temporary support system to help guide their specific deliberations.

The inquiry exercises in the earlier chapters in this book have prepared you to use the following metacognitive guide during your problem-solving efforts. Part 1 emphasizes constructivist reflection, part 2 focuses on collaborative inquiry, and part 3 concerns continuing professional inquiry. Study the following list carefully. Later you will apply it to the study of specific student learning problems.

The Metacognitive Strategy

Part 1

A particular student under my care has a learning problem. How shall I define this problem with reference to what I am trying to teach, the student's past experiences, and the student's personal purposes? In other words, how shall I frame the problem so that the student will engage in constructivist learning? What solution or solutions should I try? Do I expect my problem-solving efforts to succeed, or do I anticipate engaging in further inquiry? Does this problem challenge my curriculum and classroom community leadership thinking?

Part 2

Can I collaborate with anyone about this problem? What would be the value of such collaboration?

Part 3

Now that I have engaged in my best thinking on a specific student's learning problem, do I have any additional thoughts on my professional values? With this case analysis experience under my belt, how do I understand the concepts of educational problem solving, curriculum leadership, and classroom community leadership?

Examining Case Studies

We now turn to the study of complex cases of student learning problems. There are many different ways to engage in case analysis (Kowalski, Weaver, & Henson, 1990; McCarthy, 1989). The primary significance of a case is not the description but rather the consideration of a problem, and different people think about educational problems in different ways. You will use the three-part metacognitive strategy for your case work.

Although long accepted as a method for educating business and law students, the case study method has only recently been used in teacher education. The Carnegie Corporation's report, *A Nation Prepared: Teachers for the 21st Century* (1986), recommends that the case method employed in business schools be adapted for teacher education (McCarthy, 1989). You will now be introduced to two specific case study methods: *simulated case reflection* and *actual case reflection.*

Simulated Case Reflection

There are four simulated cases at the end of this chapter. Each describes a complex, unbounded problem in a particular type of institution. The institutions are a primary school, a middle school, a junior high school, and a senior high school. The cases follow the four-part Harvard University Business School format (Christensen, Hansen, & Moore, 1987): *Flashpoint, Background, Situation,* and *Flashpoint Reprise.* The *Flashpoint* section opens the case, catches your attention, and foreshadows the problem. The *Background* section provides the necessary contextual information, while the *Situation* section describes the problem. The *Flashpoint Reprise* returns you to the starting point of the case so that you can begin your work. The format is quite dramatic; as McCarthy (1989) points out, a "good case is good drama" (p. 16), and good drama helps stimulate your thinking.

Each case is based on information carefully compiled through lengthy interviews with an "informant teacher," who was the actual protagonist of the story. The cases, therefore, simulate true-life incidents. You should reflect on the learning problem as if you were the protagonist. As you recall from chapter 4, classroom learning situations are quite complex.

The cases can't possibly replicate the rich contextual information in real learning situations. Therefore your case analysis must be somewhat imaginative and speculative in nature. Furthermore, in simulated case work, you cannot engage in the complete cycle of active problem solving described in chapter 4. You have no chance to observe, reflect upon the consequences of your actions and, if necessary, engage in further inquiry. Nevertheless, simulated case reflection is a valuable exercise that enables you to practice the metacognitive strategy.

An Example of A Simulated Case Reflection

A secondary education student used the metacognitive strategy to analyze the sample case: "So, You'll Be Experimenting On Us." This case and the student's analysis follow.

CASE STUDY

"So, You'll Be Experimenting on Us."

Flashpoint

Mary Bloom stood by the window in the empty second-floor classroom and watched the kids from Edison High School spill out onto the street. The clock on the wall told her it was 3:25; apparently Lisa was not going to come to see her after school as Mary had requested. Running footsteps echoed in the hallway as the last few students left. Mary sat down at her desk, realizing that all this time she had been clenching the paper she had confiscated from Lisa during class. Thinking of how Lisa had once again demonstrated her lack of respect for her, Mary unconsciously crumpled the paper in her fist. Why had this particular student taken such a dislike to her?

Background

The School

Edison High School is located in a working-class neighborhood of an industrial city. At the time it was built in 1912, the brick and stone structure had won architectural awards. Now it is in a sorry state of disrepair. The walls are scarred with grafitti. The small, once-grassy campus has given way to dirt and weeds. The first-floor windows are reinforced with wire and bars.

The slow decline of Edison High mirrors the history of the neighborhood. Once a solid, middle-class enclave of white European-American ethnic groups, the economic level of the area declined as the earlier residents moved to the suburbs. The neighborhood was now a mixture of Hispanic, black, and white working poor. The student population at Edison reflects this mix fairly well, with about 50% Hispanic, 30% Black and 20% white students.

The Protagonist

Mary Bloom is a 30-year-old white English teacher, a recent graduate in her first teaching job. After getting an undergraduate degree in English, Mary worked for several years for one of the city's newspapers before returning to school to pursue a second career in teaching. An excellent student, Mary felt that she had finally found her calling. She possessed a special affinity for adolescents and was looking forward to teaching high school. Mary's teacher/mentor at Edison, where she had done her student teaching, praised her highly. She had developed a good rapport with her classes and was confident about starting her teaching career.

On the job Mary encountered a few minor problems at first, but in general her classes were running fairly smoothly. Until the situation with Lisa came along.

Situation

Mary taught three freshman composition classes, but the class she really looked forward to was the American Literature class with the juniors. The class consisted of 23 students, 14 girls and 9 boys, with a racial mix consistent with the rest of the school. Lisa Hernandez, a petite, attractive 16-year-old, had made an impression on Mary the first day. In telling the students a little bit about herself, Mary had mentioned how pleased she was to be teaching her first literature class. "So, that means you'll be experimenting on us," Lisa had said aloud, to which Mary had replied, "In a good class we should all be able to learn from each other."

Since then, nothing Mary did seemed to satisfy Lisa. She sometimes noticed Lisa smirking during class, but never being overtly disruptive. When she spoke to another teacher, Mary discovered that Lisa was a fairly bright student who was doing "A" and "B" work in her other classes. In Mary's class, however, she was only turning out average work. Challenged by Lisa's negative attitude, Mary made a point of looking at her, calling on her frequently, and trying to get her more involved. Lisa's responses in class were consistently weak and confused, usually accompanied with a comment such as, "I don't think that was explained very well," or "I don't see why we need to know that." Mary overlooked Lisa's mumbling to herself or another student, presumably about her unhappiness with the class. Because it was not obtrusive, Mary felt it best to ignore the verbal sniping. Lisa continued to turn in "C" papers that were more lackluster and careless than incorrect. The rest of the class ran the gamut from a straight "A" student to those who were doing below-average work.

Mary had decided to write Lisa off as a chronic complainer and get on with the rest of the class until that morning, when one of her other juniors had stopped by to speak to her. Nancy was the shy, quiet, 16-year-old black girl who was getting the straight "A's" in class. She seemd nervous as she approached Mary.

"Hello, Nancy. What can I do for you?" Mary said.

"Hi, Ms. Bloom." Nancy fiddled with her book. "Ms. Bloom, you know Lisa?"

"Yes, of course. Why?"

"Well, don't say that I told you, okay? She's got this paper that she's passing around the class."

"You mean an assignment she's letting other people see?"

"No, Ms. Bloom. Like a petition or something. It's about you." Mary was too surprised to respond immediately. Before she could question Nancy further, the student turned to go. "Please don't say I'm the one who told you, Ms. Bloom. I just thought you ought to know. I don't agree with it myself. I don't think it's right."

"Well, thank-you for sharing this with me, Nancy," Mary managed to say as Nancy disappeared out the door.

In class that afternoon, Mary kept a close eye on Lisa while the class worked on a writing assignment. After several minutes, she noticed that one of the boys slipped Lisa a folded piece of paper. Immediately, Mary was standing next to her.

"Let me see that paper, Lisa."

"What paper?"

"That paper that Carl just handed you."

"He didn't hand me anything."

"Look, I just saw him do it. That paper is right here." Mary pulled on a sheet of paper that Lisa had tucked into her closed textbook.

"Hey! You have no right to do that!" Lisa yelled. By now the whole class was buzzing.

"Okay, quiet now everyone! Continue with your assignment." She looked down at Lisa. "Lisa, see me right after school today."

Lisa looked down at the desk and did not respond. Mary walked back to her desk, unfolded the piece of paper, and read, "We the undersigned think that Ms. Mary Bloom is not qualified to teach American Literature to juniors. She has no prior experience and many students are not doing well in her class because she does not know how to explain the subject and how to teach. We would like to request that the administration please do something about this situation as it is unfair to the students." Even more surprisingly, the petition had been signed by six of the students. Mary recognized four names of people she had seen Lisa hanging out with in the halls. Then the bell rang and class was over.

Flashpoint Reprise

Back in the empty classroom, Mary gathered her things together. I wonder how many more of the students might have signed if given the chance? she thought. I wonder if any were asked and refused? She tried to fit the pieces together, but she wasn't sure where to begin.

*** *A Secondary Education Student's Case Analysis***

Something is definitely amiss because Lisa seems to be doing well in her other classes. I need to delve into the causes and come up with possible solutions that will help Lisa become a student of literature. I do have a great advantage as a literature teacher because I can subtly try out solutions through reading and writing assignments. I don't want to scare Lisa, or even worse, cause rebellion.

The first thing to think about is Lisa's past experience. Has she ever had a teacher who resembled me in looks or technique? Maybe she had a teacher who "experimented" on her in a previous class and Lisa is now afraid of similar treatment. One way to find out is to examine her previous grades. Another way is to have the students write an essay on one or more past teachers that they have had. This assignment could be compared to a literary work. For example, a biography on Albert Einstein could set the tone for a look at insensitive teachers. (He had teachers who could not understand his special genius.) Lisa's paper may not only give me insight into her past, it may also serve to vent frustrations that underlie the current learning problem.

Another past experience consideration would be home life. Maybe Lisa was beaten by her parents, and I somehow remind her of them. A biographical essay on the student's family experiences might provide some useful information. The problem might be rooted in Lisa's desire to rebel from a past of overly strict parenting. She may be just looking for any opportunity to have her own say.

Maybe Lisa was raised with prejudiced ideas. She might not like a white woman teaching minorities about their own cultural heritage. Her family might be very defensive of their culture and regard middle-class teachers as people who are trying to destroy their identity. A view of America as a melting pot might come in handy in this situation. Students could do biographies on the authors of their choice. This might help me understand Lisa's interests, which I could then consider when I do my curriculum planning. I might discover ways to spur Lisa's desire to excel like she does in her other classes.

If the problem is rooted in Lisa's past experiences, I could also talk to Lisa about it. Asking her not to confuse the past with the present could be a major step in alleviating the problem. If the problem is personal, however, asking for additional professional help might be necessary. One thing we must recognize as educators is the legitimate boundary of our work. We can adapt our classroom curriculum to help solve problems, but we overstep our bounds when we try to play psychologist. There is a fine line here, and the good problem solver knows when to say when.

Another major question I need to ask deals with Lisa's personal purposes. Does she really care about literature? Does she even want to be in this class? Is this an early form of senioritis setting in? Maybe she loves literature but doesn't want to be labeled a "geek" by her peers. Whatever the case, I need to research Lisa's reasoning for her actions.

When looking at Lisa's personal purposes, I need to consider her extracurricular activities as well. Does she work; and if so, does this environment promote her negative attitude towards the class? Do I need to talk with her parents and possibly her boss? Lisa may also have a boyfriend who is failing in another English class. He hates this subject, and she could be doing this for him as a "gesture of love."

Lisa could be the victim of a depressed environment. Edison is old and run-down, and that could affect the disposition of some of the students—especially those who look to school as an escape from dilapidated homes. If this is the case, a class project may be a helpful tool. The students could choose an American novel and design a big wall mural depicting one of its scenes. Art students could help paint it. This would make the book come alive and at the same time liven up the school's atmosphere.

I realize I'm raising some questions that relate to my curriculum leadership. I have to ask myself if the curriculum is part of the problem. Maybe Lisa is the only student with enough nerve to complain that my lessons are too boring or too complicated. I need to pursue this type of inquiry no matter how much it hurts my pride. I need to always remember that I am here for the children and their education.

I must consider my classroom community leadership, too. Did I set the stage for this barrage of discontentment from Lisa by comments I have made? Why does Lisa rebel only in my class? Am I being too wishy-washy in hopes of befriending my students? Do the students perceive me as standing for important community values? I need to make sure I have established credibility with Lisa, as well as the rest of the class. How does Lisa perceive me as a leader? After all, I told her to stay after school and she did not; does this tell me something about how she views me as a disciplinarian? Do I need to consider a form of discipline that helps Lisa realize that I am the classroom leader? Should I give Lisa a detention? I need to be certain that I am administering the punishment as a leader concerned about her education and not just as an authoritarian teacher exercising power. This is how I establish my role in the classroom as a fair and democratic decision maker.

Even though some of these solutions are abstract, I need to consider them as possibilities. In fact, I need to think as broadly as I can because learning problems are usually complicated. If I consider all the possibilities, there is a better chance I can hit upon a good definition of Lisa's problem, but this doesn't mean that I will be able to actually solve the problem. Teachers can only inquire and problem solve within the bounds of their capabilities and responsibilities.

Collaboration occurs when the ideas and/or opinions of others are sought. If one person can come up with lots of possibilities, imagine what two people can do, not to mention three or more. We can extend our bounds of the classroom by seeking the help of others. Social workers may be able to help if there is a problem at home. The help of the school psychologist may be needed if the problem is emotionally rooted. My judgment on a particular case may be clouded because of my close involvement. A fresh viewpoint on a situation may provide insight previously overlooked.

As I mentioned earlier, it may be helpful to collaborate with Lisa's parents. They may be able to provide important insight into the problem. I also mentioned Lisa's boss. He may have similar problems with her and may have come up with possible solutions. Above all, the person I need to try to collaborate with is Lisa. She seems reluctant to have a direct confrontation. After all, she did ditch my request to stop after school. But just the same, I need to make an effort to talk with her directly in order to understand her motives. Even if I come up dry, Lisa would know that I am hearing her and trying to resolve the conflict. Maybe I can offer her the chance to contribute ideas to the course curriculum. I just need to remember not to scare her away with an overly authoritarian tone, or give her reasons to rebel further.

As one can see, problem solving is a tough thing to do. It requires much reflection and question-raising. To explore all the possibilities as a committed professional, I need to function at a high level of inquiry. The situation with Lisa may be very complex, or it may be very simple; I just don't know. What I do know is that I need to find a solution, because Lisa is not learning literature, and this is a challenge to my job. Doctors do not play the odds and let an occasional one slip by. They try with every patient. They work within their capabilities to save all of their patients. As a professional educator, I need to do the same thing. I cannot teach the majority of my students and let some slip by. I need to exhaust my capabilities as a curriculum and classroom community leader. This requires commitment: commitment to teach, commitment to try, and above all, commitment to the future.

I need to be a good problem solver in order to do the job properly. Learning problems are always going to arise. I need to cater to all of my students—no matter what their background is. Some teachers would let

Lisa slide by, ignoring her comments, and blaming her bad attitude. In pursuit of high professional values, I need to do better. I need to consider all the possibilities when it comes to Lisa's education. I must put forth my best effort. If Lisa's problem isn't resolved, I at least know I have given it my best shot.

As I reflect back on my problem solving for Lisa's case, I think about my curriculum leadership. Maybe my course planning wouldn't be part of the problem; but I do know that a well-researched curriculum not only helps the students learn smoothly, it also inhibits them from questioning the teacher's ability.

Curriculum leadership must, of course, be coupled with classroom community leadership. Teachers must be confident not only about what they are teaching but also about how they are conducting the classroom. I need to have confidence in myself as someone who is properly and democratically leading my students. Granted, adjustments must be made as the need arises, but overall I must always remain an alert and thoughtful inspirer of important community values.

As a teacher of students who will probably have very diverse backgrounds, I am going to be confronted with situations I didn't plan for. By dealing with Lisa's problem, I become a better decision maker. Maybe I can even prevent such problems from getting started in the first place. I must remember that "an ounce of prevention is worth a pound of cure." Finally, problem solving can result in growth for me as a teacher. No matter what the final outcome will be for Lisa's case, by working hard at my inquiries I will become a more experienced reflective teacher.

Actual Case Reflection

Applying the service ideal of this book to a simulated case problem is only the first step in good reflective practice. If you have the opportunity, you should practice the metacognitive strategy on actual problems in real classroom settings. This type of systematic reflection falls under the category of *action research.* Action research is "a form of self-reflective problem solving which enables practitioners to better understand and solve pressing problems in social settings" (McKernan, 1987, p. 6). A vast amount of literature is available on the many types of action research; once you complete this book, you may want to begin to examine this literature. *Action Research in Classrooms and Schools* (Hustler, Cassidy, & Cuff, 1986) and "Teacher as Researcher," the special Summer 1990 issue of the journal *Theory into Practice* would be good places to start.

Fosnot (1989) describes a systematic way to begin reflecting on actual classroom problems. First you clinically interview individual students to gain firsthand experience with learning problems. Then you engage in collaborative reflective practice with an experienced teacher who is willing to share his or her problem solving expertise. Finally you begin your own thoughtful work.

In the following compositions, a special education student and an early childhood education student reflect on actual classroom learning problems using the metacognitive strategy to guide and retrospectively describe their reflective efforts. In contrast to the simulated case studies, actual case reflection allowed them to complete and describe the complete problem-solving cycle.

✷ *The Special Education Student's Composition*

Part 1

I am completing a field placement as a Special Education major, and I have been working with my cooperating teacher, Mrs. Harter, to solve Jennifer's learning problems. Jennifer is a four-year-old girl who has been placed in a preschool class for the deaf. She has been put in this class because she had been labeled as both blind and deaf in her IEP (Individualized Education Plan). However, based on careful observations over the past several months, Mrs. Harter has concluded that these handicaps are not the key concern. Her real learning problem seems to be her violent behavior. She bites other students and hits the teachers. She also engages in the perseverating behaviors associated with autism. Throwing temper tantrums has become part of Jennifer's daily routine. For example, she will violently throw herself on the floor while kicking, screaming and shaking furiously.

Mrs. Harter believes that Jennifer has brain damage and that this is her biggest obstacle to learning. Jennifer was born to a teenage mother who used cocaine. As a baby she spent a lot of time in the hospital and was tested extensively. The visual and hearing impairments mentioned earlier were the only problems that were found, and that's why they are duly noted in the IEP.

Jennifer's mother seems uninterested in her daughter's education. When Mrs. Harter contacted her by phone, she kept turning the conversation back to her own schooling problems. The mother rarely brings Jennifer to school on time. Jennifer's schedule is a half-day in the deaf classroom 4 days a week and a 45-minute home visit once a week. The purpose of the home visit is to help the mother interact more positively with her daughter.

At this point in our problem solving, we are still struggling to find a solution to Jennifer's violent behavior. We wonder if we have defined the problem correctly. We have begun to establish a reinforcement schedule based on specific social development goals, but we are doing this without the mother's help. Up to this point our efforts have not been that successful, so we have to keep trying and raising questions.

Part 2

Mrs. Harter has referred Jennifer's case to a teaching/administration team to see if there could be a better placement for her. Is there another class that she would benefit from more than from a deaf classroom? Mrs. Harter has proposed the idea of placing Jennifer in an SBH (Severely Behavioral Handicapped) classroom for 2 days a week and keeping her in the deaf class the other 2 days. The other possibility is to have someone with the appropriate SBH background come into the deaf classroom to work with Jennifer. The advantage of both solutions would be that Jennifer's violent behavior would be dealt with, while Mrs. Harter and I continue to work on her social development. Jennifer needs to develop her communication skills so that she can begin to interact more with her peers. At the present time, she behaves like a 6-month-old baby.

There are some other collaborative possibilities that I would like to pursue with the help of Mrs. Harter. Perhaps Jennifer's father, grandparents, or other caretakers could be brought into the picture. Why couldn't they help educate Jennifer? We could set up daily and long term goals tied to a reinforcement schedule that would be implemented at home. Our goals would be collaboratively set so that our home and school efforts would be consistent. Our guiding strategy would be to use Jennifer's good behaviors as a basis for building new social skills. Over time, Mrs. Harter and I may be able to gradually shift from a direct teaching role to a supportive position for Jennifer's home-based parenting.

Part 3

As a Special Education major learning the profession, I see it is necessary to keep up with what is happening in all areas of my field. It is possible that a student like Jennifer could be placed in my classroom where she or he is not able to benefit, or that student may display more than one handicapping condition that has to be treated.

With this problem solving experience behind me, I realize that my curriculum must be individualized, imaginative, and constantly changing to meet the needs of each child. I also realize that my classroom community leadership efforts should involve the children's parents or other caregivers as much as possible. They will then be more apt to help me teach appropriate values and behaviors for successful social interaction. I understand that much collaboration, inquiry, and perseverance are required to be a teacher of children with special needs.

The Early Childhood Education Student's Composition

A child at the day-care center where I work has a problem. He hits and throws toys. This child's name is Blaze, and he is 22 months old. He is at the day-care center from 7:00 a.m. until 4:30 p.m.. His parents have recently divorced, and he lives with his mom and his 3-year-old sister. He usually sees his dad once a week. As I understand Blaze's problem, he doesn't know how to express his feelings without being nasty.

When I first started working at the center, some of the kids acted distant towards me. Blaze was one of these children. At first, when I would change his diapers, he would get angry and fussy. I always tried to talk to him and play games with him to show that I cared. One day, Blaze put his arms up to me. I picked him up, and he gave me a big hug. I was rather surprised and very pleased when it continued to happen. He became excited when I played with him. He began to jump into my lap and pinch my cheeks. Then he began to throw toys and to hit. One day he took a bucket and hit me across the nose. At this point I didn't know what to do. He had hurt me rather badly. I wanted to punish him, but what had he really done wrong? What was the problem? At the time, I let the bucket incident slide; and now I have a problem that won't let up. He isn't a mean little boy, but I feel he hits as a way to express his feelings.

Blaze's past could be an important part of his problem. According to another teacher, his parents' divorce was quite brutal. He has probably witnessed his mother and father arguing, hitting, and generally harassing one another. Since he is so young, he may assume this kind of behavior is normal at times. Since his parents didn't get along with one another, there may not have been much warmth at home.

At this point in his life, Blaze needs certain things. To start with, he needs love, warmth and comfort. He needs to know someone is going to be there when something happens to him. When he wants to express how he feels, he needs to know that he has someone to share with. If he has a question, he needs to know that there is someone who will answer it. He is trying to develop who he is and to find all the qualities he has. As his teacher, I am trying to help him become a child who knows how to share, cooperate, communicate, interact, and constructively express feelings.

How does this problem affect who he is and what he is trying to learn? The children around him don't understand that when he pulls their hair, he is struggling with his feelings. Because of this, he misses the enjoyment and interaction of his classmates. Because he doesn't interact that well, he doesn't see the various ways the children express themselves.

What can I do as a teacher? I try to have activities that involve everyone: group stories, shared coloring activities, and games like ring-around-the-rosy. I let him be the leader when we do certain things. I let him pass out the paper and the crayons, and at times I let him pick the book we are going to read. These things help him feel important. I take him to the Baby Room and let him help me feed a baby a bottle.

Who else can I talk to about the problem? I could talk to his mom or dad, but I don't think they would help. At this point, I think they would just blame Blaze's problem on one another. I could talk to his sister and ask her what her brother is like at home. She is only 3 years old, so I would need to be quite sensitive about what I say. I have talked to several other teachers and have picked up some useful ideas.

I have begun to try several solutions for Blaze's problem. If Blaze shows his affection by pulling hair, I talk to him, explain why it is wrong, and then give him a kiss on the hand. When he jumps on me, I have him sit down alone. I say, "gentle" and explain what I mean. I let him sit next to me when I hold a baby or one of his classmates and explain to him that this is the way some people show their affection. If none of these things work after a month or so, I may have to start using time-out strategies. If I ever do begin to isolate him socially, I will be careful to explain the reasons for my actions; and I will continue to be warm and supportive. I will also design situations where Blaze can comfortably share a toy with a classmate. Eventually, I hope, he will begin to realize how to socially express his feelings.

Working with children is one of the best things in my life. I can watch them play, and I can interact with them. I can share my love for them and even my dreams. I can let them become part of me. Each day when I walk in and see them, I wonder what is going to happen. Working at a day-care center has shown me how much I enjoy helping them find solutions to their problems and answers to their questions. They are always willing to learn something new and share something old.

Problem solving is part of every teacher's life because every day there is a new problem. It seems so easy just to think of questions and solutions, but the hard part is testing them to see if they work. It is so important that your kids know you care about them. It is important that they know you are going to share everything you have inside, and that you will be imaginative and patient. This is what I am learning professionally as I work with Blaze.

Case Studies

The following four simulated cases have been designed to help you apply the three-part metacognitive strategy outlined in this chapter. Remember, these cases have been included to help you practice the book's model of inquiring, reflective teaching. Don't be too quick to define the learning problem, and try to be as inquiring as you possibly can. You may find it most fruitful to approach the case as if you were the protagonist. This was the approach the secondary education student took in the sample case analysis.

CASE STUDY

Holding Amanda Back

Flashpoint

"I've got a tummyache." Amanda, a first grader, looked up at her teacher with large, pleading eyes. "I don't want to eat."

Time for the stomachache routine again, Charlotte Porter thought to herself. But to Amanda she said, "Are you sure you don't want to try to eat? Not even a little bit?"

Amanda shook her unruly red curls decisively. The other children had already filed out to the lunchroom. "I want to stay here."

"Now you know you can't stay in here alone," Charlotte told her, as she had done at least every second day since school began 3 weeks ago. "Come on, I'll walk you down to the lunchroom."

Amanda trailed slowly behind her, looking as miserable as a six-year-old could look. Well, at least she doesn't actually get sick, Charlotte thought. Look on the bright side, it could be worse.

As she watched Amanda slowly walk over to a table and sit down by herself, Charlotte recalled the meeting she had had the previous day with Amanda's mother, Molly Davis, and Sam Anderson, the principal of Austin Magnet School.

Ms. Davis is a divorced woman in her early 40s, a librarian by education and trade. Apart from her owl-like spectacles, her appearance is somewhat flamboyant, with shoulder-length red hair that matches Amanda's. Both times Charlotte had seen Ms. Davis she had been dressed all in black, with chunky silver jewelry: large dangly earrings, and a wristful of bracelets that jangled with every movement of her arm. She was obviously intelligent and well read, and she reminded Charlotte in her appearance and manner of a 1950s style Bohemian. At their meeting yesterday, Ms. Davis had done most of the talking, her glance alternating between Charlotte and Sam as she spoke.

"Amanda has been reading since she was 3 years old," she said. "I'm sure her behavior problems occur because she's bored in first grade. She needs to be challenged. You yourself said she's reading at about a third-grade level!"

"She may be reading at the third-grade level, but emotionally and socially she's still very much a first grader," Charlotte replied.

"You shouldn't judge her on whether or not you like her personality. You're supposed to be judging her on her schoolwork. She is very well behaved at home. She just needs the proper stimulation. That's one of the reasons I wanted her to come here to the magnet school. It's unfair to hold her back when she is so clearly advanced."

Charlotte had tuned out the rest of Ms. Davis's monologue. She wondered how a child's own mother could miss seeing what the real problem was. She was brought back by the sound of Sam Anderson's voice.

"Let me assure you, Ms. Davis, Ms. Porter and I will discuss the situation and see what can be done." He ushered Amanda's mother out the door. When she left, he turned to Charlotte.

"Okay! Let's think this over and get back together tomorrow."

"What do you mean?"

"I mean Ms. Davis. If we keep 'holding Amanda back,' as she claims, she may take her out of Austin. That would be a shame."

"Yes, it would be," Charlotte agreed. "It would also be a shame to skip an emotionally immature 6-year-old up to a group of 8-year-olds, where she'll feel even more isolated than she does now."

"You don't have to give me an answer right now. Do me a favor, just think it over, all right? Then let me know tomorrow, at 3:00 p.m."

Background

The School

Austin Magnet School is located just outside the central business district of a large midwestern city. It is housed in a fairly modern, three-story glass and concrete building. Students at Austin are admitted on the basis of their standardized test scores, which must be in the upper one fifth for their age group. After that other criteria are considered, including financial resources and ethnic background. Austin admits no student whose parents make over $30,000 per year. The children are also carefully selected to maintain a diverse ethnic and racial balance. It is one of only three such magnet schools in the city, and competition for admission is intense. Because of this, most parents of students at Austin are very concerned with their children's academic progress. There is frequent communication between parents and teachers, and many parents take an active part in school activities.

The facilities at Austin are well maintained. Class size is limited, and resources are usually adequate to support the above-average status quo. A teaching position there is considered a "plum" assignment among the public schools. The faculty are energetic, dedicated, and proficient in their areas of expertise. Sam Anderson, the principal, is a youthful 45-year-old white male whose low-key but effective methods of dealing with faculty, parents, and students have earned him respect. Austin enjoys an excellent academic reputation. Students tend to be highly motivated achievers who graduate on to magnet or private high schools where they usually do very well.

Because Austin is a magnet rather than a community school, students come from various areas of the city, united by their high potential, limited family incomes, and their parents' desire for a quality educational experience for their children. All the children are either driven to school or take the school bus for transportation.

The Protagonist

Charlotte Porter, a young black woman, is fulfilling a career ambition by teaching at Austin. Charlotte attended the city's parochial schools, received a scholarship for the state university, and earned her degree in elementary education. A very successful student, Charlotte achieved high grades in her classes and discovered that she had a real knack for communicating with children. Students responded well to her, and she received excellent evaluations from her student-teaching supervisors and professors. These, combined with her energetic, positive personality, helped her to attain the position at Austin. She had been teaching there for 1 year when the problem with Amanda Davis began.

Situation

Amanda Davis is a 6-year-old girl who quickly distinguished herself on the first day of school by refusing to participate in the warm-up activities Charlotte had prepared for her class. Amanda didn't seem to be afraid, as younger students sometimes were at first. She just sulked, displaying a rather remarkable ability to resist the persuasion of her teacher and classmates. While the other students dutifully pulled up their chairs in a circle, eager to play a get-acquainted game, Amanda sat off to one side, refusing to join the group. When another little girl approached her and asked her to join them, Amanda told her to go away.

Charlotte allowed her some extra time to become accustomed to the classroom, but now, almost a month later, Amanda was still having difficulties. She reluctantly followed directions, but when the students were left to "explore" or carry out independent activities, Amanda didn't seem to know what to do. She had not made friends among the other first graders and frequently expressed her inability to relate in hostile ways. If she joined a couple of children playing with blocks, she was as likely to knock down what they had built as to build something herself. At lunchtime she habitually complained of a stomachache and insisted on sitting by herself.

The only time Amanda seemed to interact in a positive way was during the reading hour. Charlotte had quickly noticed Amanda's advanced reading skills. While the other children were struggling to master the basics, Amanda breezed through her book in one sitting, afterwards pronouncing it "baby stuff." Charlotte encouraged her to select other books from the room's bookshelves on her own, which Amanda did, but Charlotte sensed that this might only deepen the rift that already existed between her and the other children.

Then Charlotte asked Amanda if she would like to help one of her classmates during the reading session. She put her together with Sara, a little girl of East Indian parentage who was having difficulty with the text.

Amanda became a different person when helping Sara. The aloofness that characterized most of her peer interactions disappeared. She seemed to take a great deal of pleasure in the role of tutor, encouraging Sara, smiling and clapping when Sara completed a difficult passage, and patiently coaching her when she had problems.

Apart from her enthusiasm during reading time, however, Amanda continued to display the same difficulties in making friends and partaking in group projects. After the second week of school, Charlotte had called Amanda's mother to express her concern about the child's adjustment problems. Ms. Davis had seemed interested and supportive, requesting the meeting with Charlotte and the principal.

At yesterday's meeting Charlotte had been surprised when Ms. Davis stated that Amanda should skip a grade to match her reading level and that she was being treated unfairly. From that meeting Charlotte formed an impression of the kind of pressure Amanda might be under at home, and felt even more strongly that the child needed time for socializing with her own age group. Amanda was just beginning to warm up through tutoring Sara; she would lose that opportunity completely among children whose reading level matched her own.

Flashpoint Reprise

Charlotte stood outside her classroom door as the students returned from lunch. As usual, Amanda was last, walking alone. As Charlotte watched the little girl enter the room and slowly make her way to the space she had claimed for herself near the back, Sam Anderson rushed by, probably late for an appointment.

"Don't forget, today at 3:00! I'll be looking for you!" he called as he hurried down the hall.

Charlotte headed for the chalkboard. Damian, a first grader, came running up to her. "Amanda took my crayons," he said. Charlotte looked up to see Amanda, with a small fistful of crayons, methodically breaking them in half and letting them drop to the floor, one by one.

Maybe it wouldn't be such a bad idea to put Amanda in the third grade, Charlotte mused. At least then I wouldn't have to put up with this!

CASE STUDY

Too Cute for His Own Good?

Flashpoint

Angela Harper placed the telephone receiver back in its cradle and sat for a moment, sorting out the conversation she had just had with the mother of one of her students. "If you could even call that a conversation," she thought. No wonder Jeffrey was having problems in school, if this was any indication of the kind of support he was getting at home.

After almost 4 weeks of going through a frustrating cycle of failure with Jeffrey, Angela had decided to call his mother and discuss the problem. She knew that Mrs. Watson was raising Jeffrey and his two younger sisters by herself, and that she worked during the day. Angela waited until 7:00 p.m. to call. The exchange took place as follows:

"Hello."

"Hello, may I speak to Mrs. Watson please?"

"Who's this?"

"My name is Angela Harper. I'm one of Jeffrey's sixth-grade teachers. Mrs. Watson?"

"Yeah, so what?"

"Well, Jeffrey's been having some problems in school, and . . . "

"What the hell are you calling me for?"

"I thought it might be helpful if we could discuss . . . "

"Listen. Teaching the kids is *your* job. If you can't do your job without bothering me, that's your problem. I don't ask you for help with my job, do I? So don't call here again."

Angela was left holding the phone with the sound of Mrs. Watson banging down the receiver reverberating in her ear.

Background

The School

Regis Middle School is a public institution located on the near south side of Chicago. Until recently the area was populated by mostly lower and working-class black families living in single homes or two and three-room flats. There are no housing projects in the district. Because several large medical centers and colleges are flourishing in the area, a recent flurry of construction has displaced many of the former residents. Along with the new construction came an influx of middle-class professionals who are mainly white, Asian, or Hispanic. The student population at Regis is about 70% African-American, with the other 30% composed of an equal mix of the other ethnic groups. Although the school is housed in a newer building, it was cheaply constructed, and lacks updated furniture and equipment.

There has not been much gang activity at Regis, but the overall achievement scores are somewhat below average. Many students have truancy problems, and do not go on to graduate from high school.

The principal of Regis is Mr. Harrison, a dignified-looking middle-aged black man. His overwhelming concern regarding the faculty at Regis is that they not make waves. Those who make no waves are rewarded with benign neglect from the administration. They seldom see Mr. Harrison except when their evaluations are due, and those are always glowingly positive. Those whom Mr. Harrison perceives as being too demanding or too zealous incur his silent displeasure, which manifests itself in increased surprise classroom visits, excessive criticism, and lackluster evaluations.

Because Regis is a middle school, there is a lot of interaction among the teachers. However, this is almost always confined to a limited academic agenda. The "problem" of Mr. Harrison has never, as far as Angela knows, come up.

The Protagonist

Angela Harper is a 28-year-old black woman who has been teaching sixth-grade social studies in the public schools for the past four years. She loves working with children and had always wanted to be a teacher. Her own education began in a neighborhood public school. She attended a private high school and the state university. She went directly into education as her major, where she did very well both in the classroom and as a student teacher. She acquired her current position at Regis soon after graduation.

Angela has earned a reputation among the students for being firm but fair, and she is quite popular among the children. Angela believes that social studies lends itself to many exciting teaching possibilities. She enjoys teaching and constantly strives to make her classes better. However, she does so in an isolated way so as not to rock the boat. As a result, she has thus far enjoyed a fairly positive relationship with Mr. Harrison. On her own she has successfully coped with students who presented discipline problems, or who were poor academic achievers. However, she has never encountered a student like Jeffrey Watson before.

Situation

Jeffrey Watson is a 12-year-old sixth grader. He repeated fourth grade after he missed 6 weeks of class due to a prolonged illness.

Although he is a year older than most of his classmates, physically he is smaller: short, with a slight build. Jeffrey sometimes wears the same clothes to school all week, although personally he does not appear to be unwashed or dirty. Angela has never observed Jeffrey socializing with his classmates. He always seems to be alone, except when he meets his sisters, ages 10 and 9, after school to walk them home. Angela often sees him sitting in the library or reading in the lunchroom. He appears to be a quiet, serious young man. He always sits right up front in class and is very attentive. He gives the impression of being eager to be called upon and to participate in learning activities.

Based upon her observations, Angela had first concluded that Jeffrey was highly motivated and was going to do well. She was therefore very surprised when, on his first test, Jeffrey left more than half the questions unanswered. Where he did attempt to respond, the answers were vague and disconnected. His handwriting was large and loopy, with lots of smudges and scribbles. Many words were misspelled. He did not even guess at some multiple-choice questions.

Immediately after taking that first test, Jeffrey had come to Angela after class. He smiled brightly at her, yet seemed a little shy.

"I'm sorry I didn't do good on my test today, Ms. Harper," he said. "Don't be mad at me. I know I didn't do too good, but I'm going to try harder, and next time I'll do better, you'll see."

"Of course I wouldn't be mad, Jeffrey," Angela replied. "But what happened to you this time? Why do you think you didn't do well?"

Jeffrey just smiled and shrugged his shoulders. "I don't know."

"Did you study?"

"Oh, yes ma'am, I did study! I guess I just forgot or something. But I'll study harder, I'll do better next time and get an 'A'."

Except that Jeffrey never did better. There were two more tests and four more homework assignments, none of which even approached a passable quality of work. His homework had the appearance of having been hastily scribbled, and his papers were always messy and wrinkled. The tests continued to be extremely poor, with Jeffrey often barely making an attempt to respond to many of the questions.

And each time, Jeffrey came up to her, smiled, apologized, and promised to do better. Each time Angela spoke to him at length until she felt that he understood the problem. Jeffrey made a point of telling her how much he liked her class, how she was his favorite teacher, and how he didn't want to disappoint her. He seemed so sincere that each time Angela wanted to believe him. But now she had allowed the situation to go on for too long.

A little investigating into Jeffrey's record revealed that he was also doing poorly in his other classes. Yet his psychological testing done last year had shown that he possessed an intelligence that was actually slightly above average. When she approached Jeffrey's other teachers about the problem they did not seem to be overly concerned with his poor performance. They all spoke of him fondly, remarking to Angela about how "cute" he was, and how he always was trying so hard. That was when Angela decided to call Mrs. Watson, to see if she could learn a little more about Jeffrey's background and how she might address his problem.

Flashpoint Reprise

As she hung up the phone after talking to Jeffrey's mother, Angela looked at the papers she had spread out on her coffee table, intending to refer to them when she spoke to

Mrs. Watson. She gathered them into a pile, shaking her head at the untidy-looking assignments.

Well, Mrs. Watson wasn't going to be much help here, Angela mused. What should I do now?

CASE STUDY

On A Different Level

Flashpoint

Christopher Jordan watched as the forlorn figure of his student, Katie, receded slowly down the hall, silhouetted against the bright light of the corridor's west window. He turned back to his empty classroom and slammed his fist down on the desk in frustration. It just wasn't fair that he had to be the one to tell Katie that she wasn't smart enough to enroll in the class she so desperately wanted to take. Not that we'd ever come right out and make such a blunt—or honest—statement, he thought, stuffing the day's papers into his briefcase. No, we use euphemisms and code words, like "Level 1," and "Level 2" . . . as if these kids couldn't see through that!

He sighed and started down the hall, replaying in his mind how Katie had come to see him, optimistic that somehow he would be able to help her. Instead, he had to watch her hopeful smile fade while he recited the official line about which classes Level 3 students could and could not take. She had just looked down at the floor as he added, "I wish I could help you, but there isn't anything else I can do." But wasn't there? he asked himself. Had he really done everything he could do?

Background

The Community
Fawndale is an upper-middle-class suburb of a mid-size West Coast city. It is a community of tastefully elegant single-family homes and manicured lawns. The citizens are mostly career professionals: white-collar corporation officers, physicians, and lawyers. Most of the families have two parents, and the mothers are as likely to be highly educated as the fathers. Nannies are not uncommon, but many mothers have elected to stay home with the children and become full-time homemakers and community volunteers. The parents of Fawndale take pride in the excellent quality of Parker, their local junior high school, and most of them are active supporters of the institution. Because of this, many students go to Parker who might otherwise attend private schools.

The School
Parker Junior High is a public school located in Fawndale. It is a relatively new building, about 30 years old, and is very well maintained. Equipment and supplies are plentiful and up-to-date. The student body at Parker reflects the ethnic makeup of the community: about 90% white and 10% Asian or Hispanic.

Parker Junior High prides itself on its excellent academic reputation. The principal, Jane Reed, is an energetic, stately looking white woman in her late 40s. Her enthusiasm about Parker's high national ratings on standardized tests is shared by her faculty. Parker's students are also well aware of their reputation, and the school attracts many excellent young scholars from the area.

Of course, not all students are academic achievers. Parker, along with the other schools in the Fawndale district, utilizes a tracking system that assigns students into three groups based upon their standardized test scores. The groups are labelled "College Prep Level 1,"

"College Prep Level 2," and "Pre-College Prep Level 3." Level 1 includes the above-average students and numerous outstanding achievers who supply Parker with a steady stream of awards and scholarships. Level 2 is for students who may excel in some areas, but on the whole are average to slightly above-average achievers. Level 3 includes those students who have borderline-average or below-average scores on the standardized tests, and who for the most part do not intend or are not expected to go to college. The students themselves refer to the three groups as the "Brains," the "Joes," and the "Slugs."

Jane Reed wholeheartedly endorses this tracking system. Since becoming principal 9 years ago, she has seized every opportunity to expound on its many advantages to both parents and faculty. The above-average students are free to excel without being held back by less gifted classmates. These brilliant students are the pride of Parker, and many resources are poured into Level 1 programs. Level 2 students frequently become motivated to try harder to achieve Level 1 status, but they are neither artificially accelerated nor retarded by mixing with the other two groups. Much of the Level 1 equipment and some of the programs are shared with Level 2 students, many of whom go on to attend local colleges and state universities.

Level 3 students are a different story. To avoid overwhelming them academically, they seldom share in the resources or courses earmarked for the college-prep groups. Class offerings for Level 3 include few options, and courses are more likely to have titles like "Intermediate Composition" than "Reflections of Society in American Fiction."

Principal Reed adamantly supports this "realistic" system, and her enthusiasm is contagious. She enjoys the strong support of parents and faculty as she basks in the glory of Parker's many academic honors.

The Protagonist

Christopher Jordan is a 29-year-old white male science teacher. He came to Parker one year ago, thinking it would be a good compromise between the small town where he had taught for 4 years and a major urban area. He was very pleased to get the position at Parker. He liked the more sophisticated suburban atmosphere, and at first he was delighted with the modern facilities available for his biology classes.

It wasn't long, however, before the tracking system began to bother him. Although it could be exhilarating conducting higher-level activities with his Level 1 group, he detected a lack of enthusiasm, even a sense of defeat, in the Level 3 students. Surely, knowing they were tagged "Slugs" couldn't do much for their self-esteem, he thought. So he tried to compensate by making their classes more interesting and enjoyable. His efforts often met with apathy: assigned chapters unread, homework papers unwritten, challenging discussion questions answered with stony silence. It seemed only natural that he eventually redirected his best efforts to Level 1 students, who were always bright-eyed, attentive, and eager to learn more.

Despite nagging misgivings about the value, if not the efficiency, of the tracking system, Chris allowed himself to be persuaded by the forceful views of Principal Reed and the indisputable successes of the Level 1 students.

At least he *thought* he had convinced himself, until Katie Winslow came to him with her problem.

Situation

Katie Winslow is a 14-year-old freshman at Parker. She has a plain, pleasant appearance and a placid, mild-mannered disposition. Katie's standardized test scores consistently place her solidly in the Level 3 category. Her grades in English, reading, math and social studies have been fair at best. She has a low-average IQ (95), but no particular learning disability. Her neurological workup was completely normal. Katie is rather shy and quiet, and she often daydreams in class. When confronted with a question, she usually tries to respond, and never seems surprised or upset when her answer is incorrect.

Katie is the middle child of three. Her older sister, now 18, was an average student who got married immediately after graduation. Her younger sister, currently a sixth grader, displays above-average scholarship and forceful leadership qualities that sharply contrast with Katie's. The two sisters live with their parents in a comfortable (though modest by Fawndale standards) single-family home. Katie's father is an insurance executive. Her mother works part-time in a florist shop. The Winslow family, though solidly middle-class, is at the lower end of the Fawndale social scale.

Katie's parents display interest in their daughter's schoolwork and attend parent-teacher conferences together. However, all the teachers have remarked that they do not seem overly concerned about Katie's borderline performance, and they tend to make passive, defensive comments such as, "As long as Katie is happy/well adjusted/not having discipline problems, that's the important thing."

There is one area, however, in which Katie has shown marked enthusiasm and certain ability. Katie's interest became apparent in the first biology class she took with Chris Jordan. Parker's biology rooms are stocked with a variety of flora and fauna: plants, tree seedlings, parakeets, canaries, hamsters, gerbils, turtles, frogs, lizards, and an aquarium full of fish. Katie had instantly gravitated toward the animals. When Chris requested volunteers who could stay after school a few days a week to help look after the menagerie, her hand was the first to shoot up. She stayed for an hour every day to tend to the animals and took great pleasure in caring for them. The animals benefitted as well, and their living quarters were virtually spotless.

One day he remarked on her affection for the animals. Katie smiled and said, "We can't have any pets at home. I wish we could have one."

That was at the beginning of the year. Now it was late April, and students were beginning to think about the next term.

About a week prior to the current incident, Katie had approached Christopher after class. Despite her avid interest in the pets, her biology grades were as marginal as those in every other subject. Chris assumed she was going to ask about taking care of the animals next year. Instead she pulled out a list of courses offered for Level 1 students.

"Can I ask you something?" she said, smiling wistfully and waiting for an answer.

"Yes, of course, Katie. What is it?"

"Isn't this about animals?" She pointed to the class entitled "Introduction to Zoology."

"Yes." He took the paper from her hands. "But these are Level 1 courses, Katie, these aren't. . . . " he fumbled for a word. "These are the wrong classes. Do you want a list of the Level 3s?"

She shook her head. "I have one. But this class isn't there." She produced the list of Level 3 offerings and handed it to Chris, but he didn't need to look. He knew she was right.

"Do you think I could take it?" she asked. "I'd really like to learn more about the animals."

"Did you ask Mr. Wyler? He's going to teach that class."

"No, I'm afraid to ask him. He doesn't know me. Could you ask him for me? You know how much I like animals."

"Yes, I know Katie. You've done such a good job taking care of our zoo here." She smiled broadly in response to his praise. "Well, OK, let me see what I can find out. I'll let you know next week."

But what he found out frustrated him. Bill Wyler, his biology colleague, is a man in his late 50s who has taught at Parker for 25 of its 30 years. He wears a grey suit every day. (Chris and the other faculty members had wondered among themselves, was it the same suit, or did he have a closet full of them?) He always remained somewhat aloof, though he was not really unfriendly. He is a big fan of Principal Reed and the tracking system, as

Chris found out when he brought up the subject of Katie. Wyler frowned, pushed his glasses up onto his head, and put his hands up to his pursed lips in a praying gesture as Chris explained the situation to him at lunch. Wyler listened silently until Chris ended with, "Well, what do you think?"

"Hmm," said Wyler, settling his glasses back onto his nose. "Do you think she's capable of doing the work? Perhaps she is in the wrong track?"

"No, she's really not that good of a student, but I do think her love of animals might motivate her to do better than she usually does."

"Yes, but remember, even if she does, you're still talking about Level 3. I'm sure she'd be in over her head. It wouldn't be fair to her."

"I know she'd do her best. It's the only thing she's really interested in. If you were willing to take her, I'm sure Jane would let her do it."

"Well, you see, that's the other problem. Why don't you ask her? Because even if I did agree, I don't think it can be done."

"But you will agree?"

"See what Jane says first."

Chris ran up against a brick wall with Principal Reed. He explained the situation to her in her office while she attended to some paperwork. When he finished, she stopped, looked up, and replied crisply, "I understand your good intentions, but I'm afraid it's out of the question."

Chris's guard was down, and he blurted out, "But why? What harm could it do?"

"Well, Christopher, it probably doesn't seem likely that one girl in one class could do much harm. But I'm sure you're aware that if we made an exception for one student, we'd have to make exceptions for everyone. And then there wouldn't be much of a system left, would there? I'm sure you're aware that our system has been very successful. I'm afraid your student will just have to be content with some other class."

"But Wyler even agreed to give her a chance."

Reed's left eyebrow arched skeptically. Chris could tell that she knew he was, in effect, lying.

"Did he really? I'd be very surprised. But even if he did," she leaned forward for emphasis, "it's not up to the individual teacher to make such decisions. We need to have everyone's cooperation." She leaned back again. "Trust me. Your student will be happier among others of her own ability. Now, was there anything else you wished to discuss?"

No, he hadn't wished to discuss anything else. Later that evening he received a phone call from Katie's mother.

"Katie says that you're going to let her take zoology," Mrs. Winslow said. "Is that true? Can you really get her in that class? I know it's not one of her regular courses, but she would really love to take it."

"I don't know, Mrs. Winslow, I just said I would try." He didn't have the heart to tell her he had already failed.

Flashpoint Reprise

After Katie left the biology room (for the first time ever she hadn't checked on the animals on her way out), Chris headed for his car. In the parking lot he met Ellen Chung, a social studies teacher with whom he frequently ate lunch.

"What's the matter?" she asked. "You look like your dog just died."

Chris spilled out the whole story. When he finished, Ellen said, "Well, too bad her parents aren't big wheels."

"What do you mean?"

"You know. If they could throw their weight around a little bit. . . . "

Chris was dumbfounded. "Are you serious?"

"No, I'm just being cynical. Forget it."

But as Chris drove home, he couldn't forget it. He couldn't forget the look on

Katie's face. And, come to think of it, he couldn't name one student in his Level 3 group whose parents were physicians, lawyers, or bank presidents.

CASE STUDY

Is Your Class More Important Than a Man's Future?

Flashpoint

Tim Foster, stood at the front of his classroom and surveyed his group of 25 high school seniors. A few of them were on task, writing an in-class essay; the others were talking with each other, listening to radio headphones, or just daydreaming.

"Keesha! Quiet down, now, and finish your essay!" he called to one of a group of students who had gotten a little too boisterous. They laughed, and Keesha made little effort to hide her annoyance at being singled out for comment.

Tim pretended not to notice. As he looked at their faces, he silently reviewed what he knew about their lives. Keesha had been held back a year as a sophomore, the year that her father had been shot and killed in the street, an apparently innocent bystander in a gang dispute. Frederick, the gang-banger, had carried a beeper to class to keep track of business until they were banned this year. Jeremy had been caught with a gun in his jacket yesterday; when it was confiscated, he protested that he needed it for protection. Marcella had missed a few days of school last fall when she was arrested for soliciting, apparently as part of a gang enterprise. Michael had an obvious drug problem and came to school more often high than not. Monica had one baby at home and, apparently, another on the way. Up front sat Clement, one of the few serious students, whose brother had been knifed right outside of school last month when he refused to give his baseball jacket to another kid; he was still in the hospital. Tanya, whose building had burned down 2 weeks ago, was living in a transient hotel with her mother and five siblings. Maurice never knew his father, and his mother was in jail, leaving him to be raised by an older sister. Stories of promising young lives being ground beneath the wheels of poverty and hardship were depressingly frequent, not just in Tim's class, but throughout the school.

And then there was Darryl. Six-foot, five-inch Darryl Smith, who even now was sitting with his head tilted backwards, eyes closed, apparently fast asleep. Darryl, who Tim suspected was a casual drug user; Darryl, who lived with his grandmother because his new stepfather didn't like him; Darryl, who had almost single-handedly brought the basketball team into the state semifinals, providing the only taste of school pride Wright High students had ever known. Darryl, who was flunking his senior English class and seemingly unconcerned about his precarious academic situation.

Tim walked down the aisle to the dozing young man, whose desk could not begin to accommodate his long, lanky frame. "Darryl," he said loudly. Darryl's eyelids barely fluttered. Tim was careful to avoid physical contact. All the students were watching him.

"Darryl, are you sick?" he continued. Laughter erupted in the class. "He ain't sick! He's just tired!" "Hey Darryl, wake up man!" Darryl looked at Tim through bleary eyes.

"You'd better get started on that essay," Tim advised.

"Yeah, yeah." Darryl sat up a little straighter. He appeared to have neither paper nor pen. "That goes for all of you, too," Tim added, walking to the back of the room. He stood by the back door, thinking. His body grew tense as he recalled the confrontation he had had earlier in the day with Harold Carter, the phys ed teacher and basketball coach. How could Carter, even in his wildest dreams expect Tim to give Darryl a passing grade?

Background

The Community

Wright High School is located in Knoxburg, an impoverished inner-city neighborhood of a large New England city. The streets of Knoxburg resemble a war zone. The buildings are old and crumbling. Some stand vacant, windows and doors long since broken. Some buildings have been razed, leaving trash-strewn empty lots. Few trees or green lawns relieve the bleak landscape. Several newer housing projects in the area are cheaply built, poorly designed and maintained, and universally regarded as "vertical slums". Numerous shops along Knoxburg's main street are boarded up and abandoned. The residents of the community are almost exclusively black Afro-Americans. Unemployment and crime rates are high, with significant gang and drug problems. Incomes of the Knoxburg residents are low. Many are on welfare or compensation, and those who are working tend to have low-paying jobs. It is an economically and socially depressed area. With the exception of a small, dedicated core group of parents, little interaction takes place between the neighborhood residents and Wright.

The School

Wright High School is a dilapidated three-story brick building that dates back about 80 years. Grafitti cover the walls, and the first-floor windows have been permanently boarded up. Because of overcrowding, several trailers parked in the former school yard serve as adjunct classrooms for the overflow of students, who number about 1200.

Wright is a school in crisis. Standardized test scores are in the lowest percentile ranges. Discipline is almost nonexistent, although teachers spend most of their time on classroom management tasks. Student drug use is widespread, and gang activity is rampant, despite a growing list of rules forbidding the wearing of gang colors, multicolor shoelaces, baseball caps, off-center belt buckles, gang symbols, beepers, etc.

Both student and faculty absenteeism are high at Wright. An average class of 30 to 35 students has 5 to 10 missing at any given time. The average teacher misses about one day per month. The student dropout rate is over 50%. The administration of Wright is also in a crisis. Four principals have come and gone in the past 6 years. The most recent, Mrs. Claire Burns, has been in the position for 8 months.

Mrs. Burns is a serious, professional-looking black woman in her mid-30s. Most faculty feel she is totally overwhelmed in her current situation. At first she issued memos and called meetings to address the problems at Wright; faculty, students, and parents, having been through this before, were lackluster in their response. Mrs. Burns spends a good deal of time in her office, issuing periodic missives to inform teachers of her plans for the school.

The faculty at Wright is about one third black and two thirds white. Although many of the black teachers have been there for a number of years, the white teachers tend to be young and on their first job. There is not much social interaction between the white and black teachers, although the groups are not hostile. The annual teacher turnover is about 40%.

The one positive aspect of Wright is its athletic program, in particular, the basketball team. The Hawks have brought home winning records for the past 4 years and went to the state semifinals this year. Enthusiastic students crowded into the tiny gymnasium after school to watch team practice sessions. The send-off rally for the first round of the state tournament was the most exuberant display of school spirit any of the teachers at Wright could remember ever seeing. Student volunteers made decorations and hung clever banners around the school. At the rally, some of the kids recited original poems, or raps, to the team, much to the delight of the crowd. Even the faculty was impressed. Harold Carter, the head coach, had coordinated these activities. Mr. Carter is a large, physically imposing figure with a stern expression and a no-nonsense attitude. He is by far the most popular teacher at Wright. He seems to have boundless enthusiasm and encouragement for the kids on his teams. The students respond well to Mr. Carter, partly because they are happy to have found an area in which they can feel good about their achievements. Also, because Mr. Carter is a black teacher who has been at Wright about 12 years, many students find it easier to relate to him on a personal level.

The Protagonist

Tim Foster, 25, is a white first-year teacher at Wright. He originally obtained his BA in English, then stayed in college to get his teaching degree. Tim grew up across town in a mostly white, ethnic, working-class area. Because he student taught at what he had considered to be an inner-city school, Tim had felt prepared to deal with the problems he knew must exist at Wright. But after less than a year, Tim was already beginning to reconsider his vocation. Nothing could have prepared him for the apathy (and occasional hostility) of the Wright students, for the chaos of their lives, for the oppressive ugliness of the surroundings, or for the ever-present feelings of mistrust and despair he saw reflected in the other faculty members, who seldom walked outside of the building alone.

Tim was an idealist who had come to Wright feeling confident that with lots of patience, caring, and understanding, he would be able to do a good job. But his resolve had been worn down by the relentless struggle to merely get his students' attention. He often felt overwhelmed and at a loss for ways to make his English classes more accessible and interesting. No matter what he tried, it seemed, his efforts were in vain.

His morale had reached a low point in December. Just before the Christmas break, he purchased coupons good for a free hamburger at the local fast-food restaurant and gave one to each student. Although they seemed to appreciate the gesture, they were no better behaved, and a fight actually broke out in class when someone claimed another student had stolen his coupon. When Tim inserted himself between the two battling students, he was pushed and accidentally hit in the face, causing his lip to bleed slightly. An onlooking student yelled, "Come on, let's get him!" and the rest of the class laughed.

After that incident, Tim became disheartened. He got through the days by concentrating on the few good students he had in each class, the handful of kids who motivated him to keep trying. Clement, for example, had a natural talent for writing, and had even won honorable mention in a civic essay contest Tim had urged him to enter. Keeping up in school was nevertheless a struggle for Clement; Tim had realized one day with a certain shock that Clement came to Wright each morning looking for some stability and order in his life.

Talking informally to other faculty members, Tim had discovered that many had had demoralizing experiences of their own. The prevailing attitude was one of grim pessimism.

Harold Carter seemed to be just about the only teacher who had not been deterred by the conditions at Wright. Carter seldom mingled with the other faculty, usually eating lunch on the run in the gym. Tim decided to approach Carter to see if he might be able to offer some advice. But before he had a chance to do so, Carter approached him first.

Situation

The fifth of six grading reports for the year had gone out the week before. Tim was heading for the faculty lunchroom when he saw Harold Carter striding purposefully toward him. Tim smiled in greeting; Carter did not.

"You Tim Foster?" he asked in a deep bass voice. When Tim nodded, Carter stuck out his hand. "Harold Carter, phys ed"

"Yes, I know you," Tim replied, shaking his hand.

"Let me get right to the point, Foster," Carter said with a heavy sigh. "It's about your student, Smith. The senior."

"Darryl Smith?"

Carter nodded. "He's flunking your English class."

"Yes, I know."

Carter looked impatient. "Well then, Foster, let me tell you something maybe you *don't* know. Smith has a chance, a slim one, to make something out of himself. He's the big man on our team, and several colleges are interested in him."

"College?" "Darryl go to college?" The concept seemed incongruous to Tim. "I mean he—he can barely put two words together, when he even bothers to try, but . . . "

Carter cut him off. "You don't get it, do you, Foster? Look, I am talking about a man's *life* here. If he can get into college, who knows how far he could go? He's a good athlete, and this may be his only chance to pull himself out of the kind of life he has now, you see what I'm saying?"

Tim hesitated. "I'm not sure that I do."

Carter sighed again, a deep, exasperated sigh. "Okay then, let me spell it out for you. Smith won't be eligible to graduate and get into college with an "F" in your English class, now do you see what I"m saying?"

Tim just looked at him in silence.

"Ask yourself this, Foster. How important is this one class compared to being able to give a young man like Smith with a natural ability the chance to make something of his life? You can see that he doesn't get the kind of breaks in life that you got. Just what do you suppose will happen to him if he leaves here without even graduating? Is your class more important than a man's future? Think about it, Foster. I'm sure there's *something* you can do."

Flashpoint Reprise

"Okay, time's up," Tim called out to his class. "Please hand in your essays on the way out. Remember, for next week, finish reading the story we began on Monday!" His last words were nearly drowned out as the students, talking and laughing, headed out the door.

As he passed by, Darryl handed Tim a piece of paper with his name and a few lines written on it in pencil.

"Darryl, can I talk to you for a minute?"

Darryl frowned. "I got to go," he replied.

"Just one minute?"

"What for?" The young man was clearly displeased.

Tim looked down at the essay. The first line was a sentence fragment that had little relationship to the assignment.

"On this essay—I think you can do better."

"Man, I ain't got a minute for that," Darryl said, and kept walking.

Tim almost called out after him. If I told him I had talked to Carter, that would get his attention, he thought. But then what would I say?

As the next class began to file in, Tim felt a growing sense of anger and hopelessness. Carter's words echoed in his mind: "Is your class more important than a man's future?" Sure, he would like to give Darryl a break, but how far did Carter expect him to go?

Summary

You have systematically applied a metacognitive guide, or a cognitive scaffolding, to your deliberations over complex learning problems. In effect, you have practiced the model of reflective teaching that guides this text, and you have been encouraged to be reflective as an inquiring educator. Whether your practice was on the simulated cases or the actual cases, you are now in a better position to begin a career of sophisticated, caring teaching. But be patient with yourself. You will not quickly become an expert, caring teacher. You must continuously refine your reflective and inquiring abilities over several years if you want to become adept at what you have begun to practice in this chapter.

References

Carnegie Corporation. (1986). *A nation prepared: Teachers for the 21st century.* New York: Author.

Christensen, R., Hansen, R., & Moore, J. (1987). *Teaching and the case method.* Boston: Harvard Business School Press.

Fosnot, C. T. (1989). *Enquiring teachers, enquiring learners: A constructivist approach for teaching.* New York: Teachers College Press.

Haller, E. P., Child, D. A., & Walberg, H. J. (1988). Can comprehension be taught? A quantitative synthesis of "metacognitive" studies. *Educational Researcher, 17*(9), 5–8.

Hustler, D., Cassidy, A., & Cuff, E. (Eds.). (1986). *Action research in classrooms and schools.* London: Allen Unwin.

Kowalski, T., Weaver, R., & Henson, K. (1990). *Case studies on teaching.* New York: Longman.

McCarthy, M. (1989). *Teaching cases at the Harvard Business School: A model for teacher training and faculty development.* Paper presented at the meeting of the American Educational Research Association, San Francisco.

McKernan, J. (1987). Action research and curriculum development. *Peabody Journal of Education, 64*(2), 6–19.

Oberg, A., & McCutcheon, G. (1990). Teacher as researcher. [Special issue]. *Theory into Practice, 29*(3).

Palincsar, A. S. (1986). The role of dialogue in providing scaffolded instruction. *Educational Psychologist, 21*(1 & 2), 73–98.

Vygotsky, L. S. (1978). *Mind in society: The development of higher psychological processes* (M. Cole, V. John-Steiner, S. Scribner, & E. Souberman, Trans. & Eds.). Cambridge, MA: Harvard University Press.

Wittrock, M. C. (1986). Students' thought processes. In M. C. Wittrock, (Ed.), *Handbook of research on teaching* (3rd ed.) (pp. 297–314). New York: Macmillan.

CHAPTER 9

Inquiring into Teaching Professionalism

Introduction

You now have experience with a particular interpretation of teaching expertise. You have practiced the model of reflective teaching with reference to your own learning and to simulated or real cases of student learning problems. You have also been encouraged to approach your reflective work in an open-ended, inquiring manner. These experiences have prepared you to engage in one additional type of inquiry related to your professional growth. In this chapter you will examine the concept of *teaching professionalism,* particularly as it pertains to your own development as a teacher.

Teaching Professionalism

Teaching professionalism can be understood by studying both what it is and what it isn't. Sockett (1983) states that professionals are *"principals rather than simply agents-for-others* . . . [who] have a distinctive code of ethics focusing on the interests of clients" (p. 27). Let's examine Sockett's definition in light of your work in this book. You have learned that becoming a student of your own teaching requires skill in reflection and inquiry. In chapters 3 through 8 you inquired into your teaching as an independent, active learner. You were the "principal" for your own understanding of teaching—not an "agent" for someone else's definition of teaching. In short, you were empowered to explore and discover your own meaningful interpretation of "good teaching." You experienced "empowerment-as-enablement," which Marshall and Sears (1990) describe as follows:

> Teachers become empowered or enabled in different circumstances, for different reasons, and in different ways. Their power is created and realized by them—not received from or bestowed by others. [Empowerment is, thus, interpreted as] a deeply personal process of meaning making. This model of empowerment further recognizes that one's realization of power is a process begun but never completed. When teaching is viewed as a fundamentally dynamic and political act, the folly of static "empowerment packages" becomes evident and the concept of "lifelong learning" becomes a reality. (pp. 17–18)

Though this book is designed to empower you to be the principal or master of your own professional fate, you have been encouraged to develop your teaching abilities *with reference to* a "code of ethics focusing on the interests of clients" (Sockett, 1983, p. 27). This code of ethics is the ideal of educational service inspired by Noddings' (1984) ethic of caring. You have been challenged to teach specific types of curriculum content from the perspective of your students' past experiences and personal purposes. This is complex professional work, but it is personally very rewarding. In effect, you have been developing a teaching professionalism consistent with Sockett's definition of a professional as one who is "principal" with a client-oriented "code of ethics."[1]

You may not agree with all aspects of this interpretation of *teaching professionalism*. In the spirit of inquiry, you are welcome to question or refine this particular definition to fit your own goals and values. But if you reject it completely, with what will you supplant it? What will be your definition of good teaching? Without a definition, you are functioning without professional values. Perhaps you know teachers who operate without such values. Do you respect them? Were they once service-oriented, in some sense of the term, but have since lost their way? Why did they lose their service orientation?

A key purpose of this book is to help you inquire into the type of *good* teacher you want to become. You are not studying a training manual; you are engaging in a systematic examination of a professional ideal—an ideal inspired by Noddings' (1984) ethic of caring.

Two concepts are often mistaken for teaching professionalism: *semi-professionalism* and *professionism*.

Semi-Professionalism

A professional work environment supports responsible, autonomous problem solving. In contrast, a semi-professional or quasi-professional work setting is carefully controlled through top-down accountability policies. Throughout the 20th century, public teaching has generally been organized as semi-professional work (Callahan, 1962; Foster, 1986). Teachers have been "scientifically managed" to behave in accordance with predetermined administrative policy. This is a "power over" organizational approach (Sergiovanni, 1990) in which "the situation is . . . 'defined' according to the *interpretation* of the organizationally most powerful person (Lacey, 1977, p. 73). The teacher accountability movement of the 1970s and early 1980s followed the principle of top-down management (Darling-Hammond & Berry, 1988). Lieberman (1988) refers to this as the "first wave" of teacher reform, in contrast to the "second wave," which focuses on teachers' professional empowerment (p. vii).

This administrative approach to teacher reform can also be described as a form of *bureaucratic accountability* in which "teachers are viewed as functionaries . . . separated into egg-crate classrooms and isolated [from one another] by packed teaching schedules" (Darling-Hammond, 1988, p. 11). Think back to your experiences in classrooms, both as a student and now as a student of teaching. What is the nature of the teaching work in these classrooms? Is it bureaucratic or is it professional? Now think back to your inquiry work in this book. How did you treat yourself—as a future autonomous professional, or as a future bureaucratic laborer?

Teachers are not the only workers who have been treated as semi-professional functionaries. Most work in the 20th century has been organized on the principle of bureaucratic accountability (Apple, 1982; Bowles & Gintis, 1976). This managerial approach is supported by the following rationale: "(a) individuals dislike and wish to avoid work, (b) most people work to avoid responsibility and have little ambition, and, therefore, (c) coercion is necessary" (Marshall, 1988, p. 10). In addition, bureaucratic management is often justified by a rationale that certain individuals should have *power over* others.[2] Assume for a moment that you were a top-down manager, and you wanted to ensure that the next generation of citizens in your society knew their proper place as unquestioning semi-professional workers. Wouldn't you want the teachers in your society to think of themselves in quasi-professional terms and, in turn, to treat their students as future semi-professional workers?[3] In this way you could ensure the continued supply of a docile work force that would not challenge your "power over" status. Now assume the opposite. Suppose you were a national leader dedicated to the vision of a participative democratic society in which power is shared equitably. How would you treat the teachers in your society? How would you want these teachers to treat their students? What would be your attitude towards this book?

Professionism

Professionism is a work ideology that is strictly oriented towards status, power, and money. While professionalism is based on a service ideal, professionism results from "self-serving efforts of privileged groups to preserve a mystique, to delineate a monopoly, to resist access to their ranks, to resist external controls" (Judge, 1988, pp. 229–230). Many current advocates of teacher reform argue that teaching should be modeled after the work of doctors and lawyers. But to what degree is their work service oriented, and to what degree is it self-serving? Are doctors and lawyers good models for teachers—particularly with reference to the caring, inquiring teachers that serve as the inspiration for this book? Metzger (1987) ends his analysis of professionism in modern societies with the following piece of wisdom:

> If I were to offer words of counsel, they would come down to these—that the next time you meet a professional, you would be well-advised to keep one hand on your wallet and, with the other, tip your hat [as a sign of respect for the service they provide]. (p. 18)

You don't have to "keep one hand on your wallet" if you are being served by a teacher whose work is guided by an ethic of caring. You only have to be willing to be challenged to become your "best self." But perhaps this is too idealistic a view of teaching for an imperfect, power-hungry world. What do you think? Certainly caring, inquiring teachers must be as politically aware as their more cynical peers. Keep this point in mind as you explore the topic of empowered political inquiry.

Professionalism in Practice

Today many educational organizations are promoting teaching professionalism. In fact, there is widespread interest in teacher empowerment in the United States.[4] You may be wondering how schools would have to change in order to accommodate this work ideal. In this section we will examine an elementary school and a secondary school that support professional teaching.

The Angier Elementary School

Roland Barth describes the Angier Elementary School in his book *Run School Run* (1980). Barth was the principal of this K-6 school for 6 years, and his book provides a detailed description of his school leadership. Angier is located in Newton, Massachusetts, a suburb of Boston. When Barth began his principalship the faculty was divided into two political factions; like the teacher-characters in this book, each faction had very strong beliefs about educational service. One group believed that highly structured classroom activities were the answer to good teaching, while the other advocated more open, child-centered instruction. Each faction had its own network of parental support, and friction and disagreement were common between the two groups. Barth faced a situation in which student welfare was taking a backseat to adult egos. In other words, Barth had to confront the Angier school community's own brand of teaching professionism.

Barth also had to face the tradition of scientific management that school administrators are expected to uphold. He decided to reject this tradition because, in his view, it perpetuates a downward cycle of infantilism: "School boards infantilize superintendents; superintendents, principals; principals, teachers; and teachers, children" (Barth, 1980, p. 170). Barth was fortunate in that he worked in a school district where he could create an alternative organization to better serve the educational needs of the Angier school community. His book is essentially the story of how he worked with faculty and parents to construct such a school operation.

Space does not permit a complete accounting of the Angier Elementary School story. Suffice it to say that Barth's leadership for teaching professionalism was successful. By establishing a non-divisive and broadly inclusive approach to professional service, he was able to encourage the two school factions to begin to work together. (The service ideal of this book has been similarly designed to be inclusive and non-divisive.) Over time the Angier community established the following collaborative procedures to support responsible teacher autonomy.

1. Classes can be taught by one or two teachers. (One teacher works with approximately 24 students, and two teachers work with approximately 48 students.)
2. Classes can have up to three grades of cross-age groupings (e.g., K–2, 1–3, 2–4, and so on).
3. Teachers meet with the principal each March to discuss the professional challenges they want to undertake the following school year. For example, a sixth-grade teacher who is feeling "stale" can negotiate

switching to first grade or staying with the sixth graders but experimenting with a new science curriculum.

4. Teachers create a personalized curriculum plan for each school year. These plans must be submitted to the principal for review during the early part of summer vacation.
5. Teachers collaborate with one another, with the principal, and with parents on the placement of each child. All concerned parties follow elaborate policies that involve collegial and parental classroom supervision, extensive conferencing, and procedures for public justification.
6. Each teacher is provided with a budget to purchase his or her own curriculum materials. No one is forced to use district-adopted texts.
7. Each year the principal asks individual faculty members to serve as coordinators for specific subject areas. The faculty coordinators "keep . . . abreast of each teacher's written curriculum through frequent conferences, classroom visits, and familiarity with individual curriculum outlines" (Barth, 1980, p. 101).
8. Collaborative in-service activities are tailored to fit the personal-professional development needs of each teacher.
9. Parents meet with teachers twice a year to review portfolios of student work. Teachers prepare written student progress reports to accompany these biannual teacher-parent conferences, and each report is reviewed by the principal prior to each conference.

As you can see, Barth worked hard to establish a work environment that empowered teachers to function as autonomous, service-oriented professionals.

Central Park East Secondary School

Central Park East, a New York City high school, is part of the Essential School Movement in the United States. A brief overview of this movement will clarify the organizing principles at Central Park East.

The Coalition of Essential Schools was created in 1984 through foundational and professional association support. The Coalition was inspired by several national studies that criticized the organization of secondary education in the United States. The most significant of these studies was Sizer's *Horace's Compromise: The Dilemma of the American High School* (1984). This study chronicled serious problems in the modern comprehensive high school and recommended dramatic institutional reform. These recommendations served as the basis for an alliance of approximately 45 private and public secondary schools in the United States and Canada. The common beliefs of these schools are stated as follows:

> The common principles of the Coalition . . . focus our attention on a limited number of important features of schooling: the school's purpose should be to help students learn to use their minds well; the school's goal should be that each student master a limited number of essential skills and areas of knowledge; the academic and social goals of the school should apply to *all* students; teaching and learning should be personalized; the student is to be the worker and the teacher more of a coach; the diploma should be rewarded on the basis of demonstrated competence; the school's norms should emphasize trust, decency, and unanxious expectation; the faculty should view themselves as generalists rather than specialists; and the budget should permit total teacher loads of no more than 80 pupils, while staff salaries remain (or become) competitive and total expenditures remain fairly constant (i.e., they are not to increase more than 10 percent beyond current cost-per-pupil). (Houston, 1988, p. 110)

By operating according to these beliefs, the Coalition schools have radically altered their institutional operations. Though no two Coalition schools have exactly the same organizational structure, they all share several common features. The school principal functions less as an administrator and more as a member of a leadership team that includes school faculty. This team makes all significant school-based decisions and establishes the policies for educational standards and methods of assessment (Houston, 1988, p. 110). The professional staff collaborates regularly. For example, the teachers are usually organized into four-member interdisciplinary teams that are responsible for 80 students for the entire school day. No teacher works with more than 20 students at a time, and the team members (each of whom specializes in one of the four "essential" subjects: English, social studies, science, and mathematics) meet daily to coordinate their activities. The instruction is highly personalized. Typical high school services such as athletics, extracurricular activities, or vocational programs are cut back or eliminated if they interfere with the professional work of the teachers.

Central Park East is an Essential School for grades 7-12 enrollment. This teacher-run school professes the following educational philosophy: "We looked upon Dewey, perhaps more than Piaget, as our mentor. . . . We also saw schools as models of the possibilities of democratic life" (Meier, 1987, p. 36). Meier summarized Central Park East's organization as follows:

1. All educational professionals, including the librarian and the principal, teach.

2. The educational professionals supervise one another. No outside district supervisors work at this school.
3. The school is organized into "Houses" of 80 students, and each House has four teachers.
4. Class size never exceeds 20 students.
5. To ensure personalized educational services, teachers and students in a House stay together for two years.
6. The entire school faculty has twice-a-month curriculum meetings.
7. The teachers in each academic department have a three-hour curriculum meeting each week.
8. The four-member interdisciplinary House teams take a daily 80-minute lunch together to coordinate their efforts.
9. The curriculum is designed by the teachers.
10. The curriculum schedule is flexible and can be altered to meet emerging instructional purposes. Administrative needs never dictate the schedule.
11. Curriculum resources can be purchased from teacher-determined sources. Teachers are not bound to district-adopted texts.
12. Parents meet with teachers twice a year to review portfolios of student work. (Meier, 1987, p. 37)

In sum, the teachers at Central Park East work in an organization that supports responsible professional autonomy.

The Puget Sound Educational Consortium

The Puget Sound Educational Consortium is a significant center of teaching professionalism. This network consists of 14 school districts in the Seattle, Washington, area that work with the School of Education at the University of Washington. The Consortium is dedicated to the following belief: "Teachers are experts with special talents and a deep commitment for educating new generations. That commitment is best accomplished in a professional, collaborative environment."[5]

Angier, Central Park East, and the Puget Sound Educational Consortium are examples of professional teaching settings. Perhaps there are such educational institutions near you.[6] If you can acquire field experiences in such a work environment, it will help you appreciate the value of the reflective and inquiry exercises in this book.

Professionalism in Progress

Two national policy initiatives currently promote professional school settings. Most of the major institutions of higher education in the United States have, for the first time in this country's history, joined together to reform teaching and teacher education. The group they formed is called The Holmes Group. In January 1990 The Holmes Group decided to create Professional Development Schools (PDS) as the central vehicle for their reform efforts. These schools will be designed to support teaching professionalism as it is described in this chapter. The Holmes Group report, *Tomorrow's Schools* (1990), provides a detailed description of the PDS concept.

The American Federation of Teachers (AFT) has composed a policy book entitled *Professional Practice Schools: Building A Model* (1988). In this book Levine (1988) describes the threefold mission of the professional practice schools as follows:

1. To support student learning.
2. To support the professional education of teachers.
3. To support inquiry directed at the improvement of practice. (p. 7)

The AFT is currently helping to create the first generation of professional practice schools.

You may want to inquire further into these two major policy initiatives, both of which promise to play a significant role in the movement toward teaching professionalism.

Inquiring into Your Teaching Professionalism

The final inquiry exercise of this book focuses on the topic of your evolving teaching professionalism. This type of inquiry involves the examination of three topics that are part of the definition of teaching professionalism presented in this chapter. These three topics, which are phrased as questions, are:

1. In your everyday relations, have you been and are you encouraged to engage in your own meaning making on any topic? In other words, when you interact with others, have your interpretations been respected, and are they respected?

2. In your everyday relations, have you been and are you encouraged to be the master of your own fate? With reference to your professional growth, are you being supported to become a lifelong student of your own teaching—the master of your own professional fate?
3. In your everyday relations, have you been and are you encouraged to not be overly egocentric but to look at things from the other person's point of view? Have you learned the value of the saying, "Walk a mile in my shoes"? With reference to your professional growth, are you learning an educational service ideal that incorporates students' past experiences and personal purposes in the learning process?

In chapter 3 you were introduced to five general inquiries associated with reflective practice and educational inquiry: *remembered anecdotes, role models, personal metaphors, community referents,* and *teaching discourse.* You applied these inquiries to the topics in chapters 4 through 6. We will now use these categories to explore your evolving teaching professionalism.

Remembered Anecdotes

Think back to your past everyday social relations with your parents, your teachers, your priests or ministers, and so on. Did they encourage you to engage in your own meaning making, or were your points of view, feelings, and ideas disregarded? Were you treated as someone who had power to voice an opinion on topics, or were you encouraged to be passive, docile, and dependent on others' interpretations of events? Have your perspectives on teaching met with respect? Have you been encouraged to become a lifelong student of your own teaching? Have you learned to form opinions that are not overly egocentric—that are respectful of other people's points of view? Are you learning how to teach in a way that will be respectful of your students' past experiences and personal purposes?

Role Models

With reference to the question of your personal meaning making, your lifelong learning, and your ability to understand and respect others' perspectives (others' meaning making), were you exposed to any past positive or negative role models? What did you learn from the positive role models? What did you learn from the negative role models that you may have to unlearn? Can you serve as a role model of empowerment for your students?

Personal Metaphor

Create a cluster with the term "teaching professionalism" as your nucleus. What personal metaphors appear in your cluster? In terms of the three key concepts of teaching professionalism (empowered meaning making, lifelong meaning making, and client-oriented ethics), do these metaphors serve you well? Can you imagine any new images that would help you feel more empowered? Review the personal metaphors in your cluster. Select one or more of the positive images and compose a brief expressive essay that expands on this metaphor.

Community Referents

How might teaching professionalism, as defined in this chapter, contribute to community values? For example, how might empowered teachers contribute to the health and vitality of our nation, our local schools and communities, and your future classroom community?

Teaching Discourse

Consider the discourse on teaching that you have encountered in your past as well as in your present circumstances. With reference to the norms of professional empowerment, is any of this discourse limiting? Does any of this discourse overtly and/or covertly support some form of social injustice, such as racism or sexism? Can you improve on any of this discourse? Can you imagine ways of talking about teaching that better affirm the norms of professional empowerment?

A Sample Professional Empowerment Inquiry

A preservice secondary education student composed the following essay addressing the five inquiry categories.

✳ ***Anecdotes***
Many of the power-related experiences in my life concern how I dealt with guidelines and rules. My earliest problem solving was as a child trying to get what I wanted within the established rules. As I got older and wiser, I realized that by establishing myself as responsible, dependable, level-headed and intelligent, I was able to gain further maneuverability and head more directly towards my goals.

For instance, if right after I was hired as a bookkeeper, I had pointed out to my boss that paperwork was being handled incorrectly, I would probably not have been taken very seriously. Moreover, I may even have been seen as irresponsible and labelled as a rebel unwilling to work within established rules. However, after working with the company for a year, not only have I shown myself to be productive and responsible, but my boss now has enough confidence in me to listen to my ideas. Still, I had to either keep my feelings to myself or suppress them for a period of time while I learned the framework of the company. Some people are power hungry and consequently will not share ideas easily; but if you acknowledge their tenure, experience, and knowledge (or other source of power and influence), they weaken their defenses towards you—despite themselves!

You might think my initial approach is "sucking up", but it isn't really. "Buttering someone up" suggests that one tells untruths to win the affection and confidence of another. However, my technique is to bide my time so that I can define the limitations I must work within so as to not make a big issue out of a potentially controversial subject. This is nothing more than what I do at a cocktail party: I approach sensitive issues gradually to avoid insulting anyone. Furthermore, as I get to know others at the party, I may become part of a group whose members have similar views, allowing for deeper, more meaningful ideas to be interchanged.

As I reflect on my own personal struggles to state my opinions *and* to respect the opinions of others, I can better understand why I was relatively ineffective at swaying my parents. I was only a naive child against two adults!

Role Modeling

One of my most influential role models has been one of my professors. From his stories of teaching in the classroom, I have come to see how his vision of improving teaching and teachers has led him from the high schools to the colleges. He seemed to figure out that teachers could perhaps be best helped in preservice education, rather than won over later. I imagine that this realization and the efforts to adapt to it probably happened over a number of years—years filled with frustration and disillusionment, no doubt. Still, he kept trying to find a better way to make teaching more meaningful for himself and for his peers.

His perseverance impressed upon me that entering into education—or for that matter any field—is not an end in itself, but the beginning of growth. You begin the journey with a destination—an ideal—of where you want to end up; and as you take each successive step, you guide your path to adapt to changing circumstances. A mountain climber faced with a wall of stone may not have the tools available to climb it, so he must find another path to reach the top. His climb may be longer, but his achievement will be the same. In teaching, the adaptations are more political than physical, but the mountain can be conquered just the same. As I enter my teaching career and am faced with what sometimes will seem to be overwhelming frustration and discouragement, I will remember this professor of mine: his strategizing, perseverance, and desire to improve education.

Of course, there have been negative role models in my life. In fact, I see many of these every day where I work. These people are salesmen, buyers, machinists, secretaries, credit managers, and even executives. Many of them, regardless of their earnings or status within the company, haven't realized that they are the ones in control of their lives. No one dictates to you what attitude to have, or how you must react to circumstances. Still, these individuals subject themselves to the belief that even the smallest things are outside their reach or control. They are bitter and unhappy, not only about the company, but also about their jobs. It's sad to see people relinquish all efforts at creating a job within which they can function and be happy. That is what working towards your ideals is all about—personal satisfaction. These people are soured on themselves because they have let go of that struggle. How can you justify to yourself that your ideals are second to what may be the arbitrary choices dictated by those who are higher up? Wouldn't this choice indicate that you think less of yourself than others? How can you ever hope to achieve anything without being true to yourself in your endeavors?

Personal Metaphor

Here is a cluster I've created around the nucleus of "teaching professionalism." [See Figure 9–1.] I've also composed the following expressive paragraph.

Manipulating the System

One of the most important idiosyncrasies of "systems" is that rules perpetuate themselves. Rather than seeing a particular rule as a past resolution to a problem, people see it as a sacred entity unto itself. What happens as a result is that people lose sight of the rule as only one alternative. Test this premise by challenging a rule and listening to how people defend it. They'll say things like, "It's always been done this way." They don't defend the rationale as much as the casing it's neatly packaged in: THE RULE! If you can uncover the problem that begat the rule, you have a starting point for developing a rationale for your new alternative. Then, you need only learn how to package it to sell, by establishing yourself as a responsible seller who is willing to band together with others for support. People on lower levels within the system may be more supportive than people on higher levels because they have less to lose. Of course, a democracy means that even individuals on the lower level who band together should have a voice. Behold the power that blue-collar unions have with white-collar management!

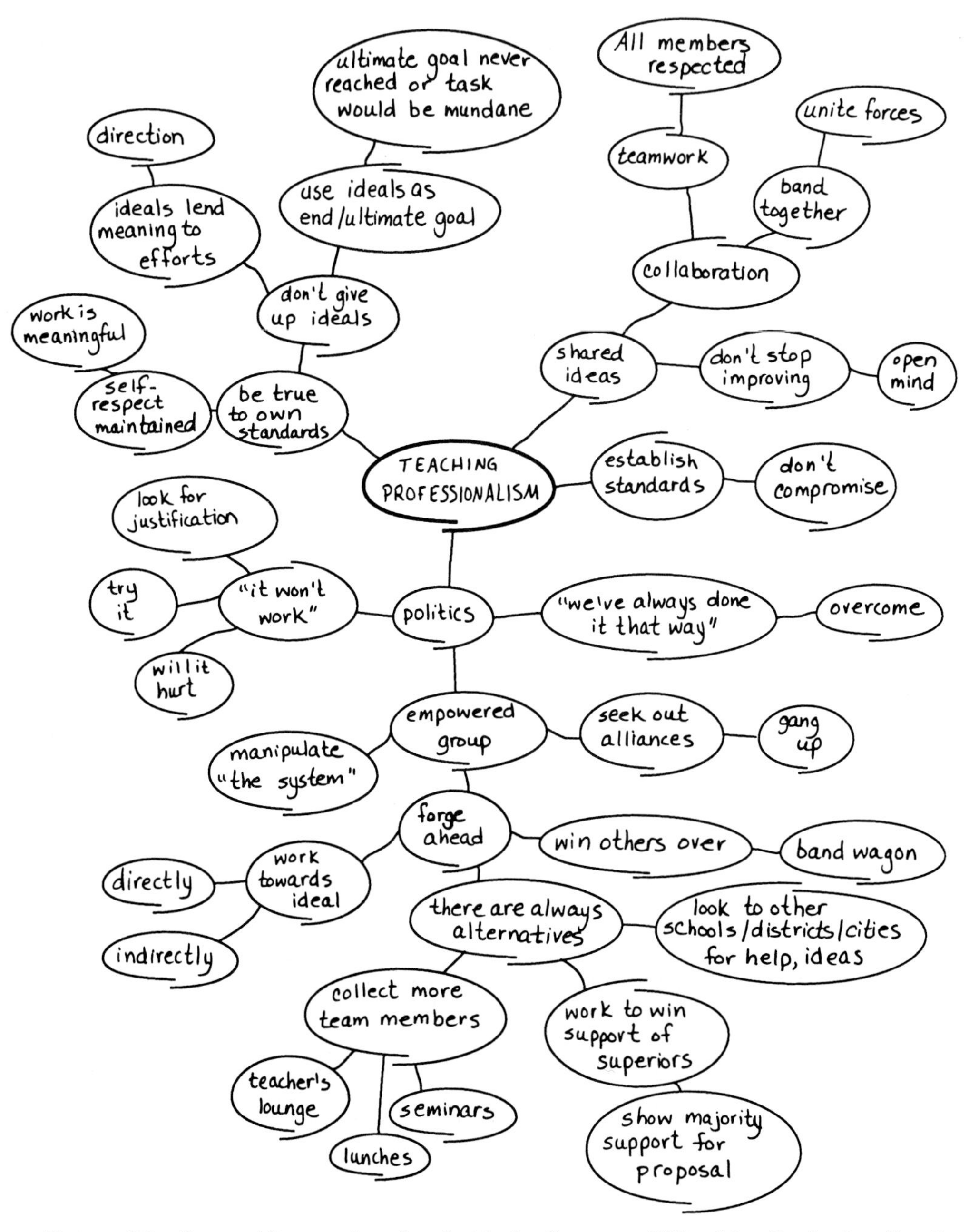

FIGURE 9-1 Personal Images Associated with the Concept of "Teaching Professionalism."

✱ ***Community***

If teachers worked towards their ideals together, they would gain more power over their lives. Teachers would see success more as a function of their own decisions and efforts. By feeling more in control of their own classes, teachers would be more willing to accept greater accountability for their actions, which would heighten the respect society has for them. It is ironic that in most professions, autonomy and individual effort are givens for successful work, yet in education teachers are lumped together into a standardized melting pot.

It seems only logical that, as a future teacher, I try to work towards the empowerment of educators. Of course, I can't do this single-handedly. Our society needs to realize that teachers have unique sets of skills that enable us to approach the challenges of teaching in different ways. We should not be asked to limit ourselves to predetermined approaches that only handicap the educational process in our classrooms.

Not only can teachers become a power to be reckoned with at lower levels, they can rise through the ranks and thereby gain more power. In both ways, teachers can help the re-evaluation of obsolete strategies. Part of what may influence educational change is the growth of teacher accountability. Accountability represents shared responsibility for success and failure; it refers to teamwork sharing between teachers, administrators, and the community. Teacher accountability would take the pressure off administrators for making classroom decisions about things they are distanced from in the first place. For instance, I know of one district whose science department purchased new biology textbooks recently, and I have heard sharp criticism by teachers in three different schools. Ironically, these teachers don't even know who chose the book; they only know that it was "some administrator." Isn't this ridiculous? We are working against each other. What we need in order to contribute the most to our communities—and to gain their respect—is professional collegiality.

Teaching Discourse

When I enter my student teaching, I will have not only the administrator to consider, but a cooperating teacher as well. I may have to play the game. If he says that loosely structured labs are a waste of time and the problem-solving skills they develop are unnecessary, what do I do? Instead of doing an entire problem-solving lab, I might include some problems in the homework assignments. This technique shows respect for the cooperating teacher's opinion while allowing me to grow professionally in ways I believe are important.

The importance of not compromising myself also means that my cooperating teacher will get exposed to my innovative ideas, too, maybe finding them to be more worthwhile in practice than he previously believed.

During my teacher induction, I will have a greater opportunity to be myself. I won't have the constant supervision of a cooperating teacher, but I will have more administrative pressure than a tenured teacher. At this point, I'll still have to comply with conservative viewpoints, but I'll have more freedom to incorporate my own ideals—though probably not outright and openly. Even then, I won't be able to do much to influence my peers; but I'll still be continuing to work towards my ideals as the specific situation allowed. For example, if the administration was not supportive of formats like cooperative learning, I could still use some group activities; they would simply have to play second fiddle to more accepted techniques.

The next step is after my tenure. After I have been accepted by the administration, I can begin to develop in accordance with my professional ideals. Yes, I may have a department head who may disagree with me, but the job security pressure is off. Still, my efforts will be pretty self-contained. I'll be developing and trying things out in my classes, feeling my way towards achieving my personal ideals for my students. At first, I won't have enough experience with the system to begin to collaborate over professional empowerment goals. I'll be wrapped up with using collegiality as a means for brainstorming lesson plans, tests, labs, group projects, and so on. Finally, though, I will get enough experience to work with others to achieve our mutual ideals.

Eventually, I'd like to be a department head or some other administrator. I wouldn't want to do this until I had developed professional collegiality with my peers. Collegiality is the springboard to greater understanding (if you participate with an open mind) and a door to a wealth of ideas through brainstorming with others. I hope that others certified before me will help me to learn how to deal with the system as an empowered teacher, and I hope to help support others who enter the field after I do. It's a matter of seeing the opportunities available and taking them. A simple idea . . . but a lot easier said than done.

Considering Solutions to Empowerment Disruptions

As you gain experience with the questioning methods of this text, you will be better prepared to provide leadership for professional empowerment. Unfortunately, many teachers think of their work in semi-professional terms (Lortie, 1975). Equally lamentable, many practicing teachers mistake teaching professionism for professional empowerment (Sykes, 1987; Devaney & Sykes, 1988). By becoming a caring, inquiring teacher, you are practicing a service ideal that can help unite teachers as true professionals.

Our country needs teachers who will help lead the fight for teaching professionalism. If you work in an institutional environment that does not support your development as an empowered professional, consider these two questions:

1. How can I become an adept problem solver when confronted by "power over" administrators and administrative policy?
2. How can I develop a support group that will help me develop as an empowered professional?

The first question is particularly relevant if you are not a practicing teacher. If you are about to go through the processes of student teaching and professional induction, you may find three problem-solving strategies useful. Goodman (1988) calls these strategies *critical compliance, accommodative resistance,* and *transformative action.* His description of these three strategies will be adapted for our inquiry purposes.

Critical compliance is the least radical strategy. When you are critically compliant, you examine disruptions to teacher empowerment in your everyday relations; but you don't immediately try to alter your circumstances. Instead, you bide your time until you are more politically secure (for example, until you become tenured). Though you don't exhibit empowered behavior, you engage in the necessary critical inquiry to keep your hopes alive and to prevent yourself from being co-opted by a disempowering system. Then, when you have established the necessary political base, you can begin to act. Goodman (1988) describes one student teacher who followed the district's phonics approach to reading but remained critical of this mandated curriculum. In effect, she patiently waited for the day when she could teach in accordance with her best professional judgment. She remarked:

> I don't know if grouping words by phonics is the best way to teach spelling. We [adults] don't learn to spell by having it on a list, writing it three times, and then having a test over it. Usually, if people read [and write] a lot, they will learn to spell. (Goodman, 1988, p. 32)

Accommodative resistance is a step up in political engagement. In this case you continue to publicly comply with school policy, but you look for small ways to function as an empowered professional. For example, you find ways to facilitate constructivist learning while still following your school district's mandated skill instruction (which is usually controlled through the administration of standardized tests). Goodman (1988) describes an *accommodative resistant* strategy that several student teachers used to supplement the morning lessons they were mandated to teach:

> Several student teachers brought in instructional games they had developed. For example, Joan set up a learning center board game that

> helped children (first and second graders) recognize antonyms, homonyms, and synonyms. The children were told that they could play this game after they had finished their morning work. (p. 33)

The final strategy is *transformative action.* You begin to take major steps to transform the work you do as a teacher—either as a single political agent or in a coordinated effort with others. For example, you develop teaching units that directly challenge the mandated curriculum of the school district. Equally significant, you are willing to publicly defend your alternative classroom curriculum leadership. Or, you might work with other teachers to develop a meaningful peer coaching and collegial supervisory system as an empowering substitute for the current administratively mandated supervision. A third example would be to devise collegial professional development activities as alternatives to the school district's typical in-service offerings.

Consider how you might apply these three strategies to your own career as an empowered professional. Can you think of any other strategies that might be useful? Critical compliance, accommodative resistance, transformative action, and other potential empowerment strategies will be difficult to practice if you are not part of a professional support group. The secondary education preservice student who inquired into her teaching professionalism describes how she has already begun to create her own support group:

> ✷ One of my most important priorities is networking to provide myself with a supportive base. My peers will help to encourage me, brainstorm with me, and advise me. I, in return, will make myself available to help them. Together we can support each other as we grow more knowledgeable through pursuit of our personal educational ideals.
>
> Setting up my own support group began as easily as trading phone numbers with my fellow students. At first, it was natural to do this in case either of us missed class, but the action soon took on more significance. I found myself talking over my philosophies of education with my peers, and we also talked about how much we could use some peer support during student teaching. Soon I found myself with a group of students who, like myself, wanted to band together.
>
> As I did the required field experience hours, I became acquainted with many teachers. I looked for support from many different types of teachers, and I have found some. I also keep my eyes and ears open. I've met teachers in restaurants, at wedding receptions, and at alumni functions. In fact, my wedding photographer was a moonlighting teacher. He was so eager to encourage me that, when I bumped into him at a friend's wedding reception, he took a lot of time to share his teaching experiences with me.
>
> Teachers are like air. They are everywhere, and they always seem to be supportive and open. I find it amazing to listen to the inspiring

stories some of these teachers have shared. My parting note is always, "Would you mind if I gave you a call sometime?" I haven't had anyone say "no" yet.

Conclusion

You have now come full circle with the inquiry work in this text. You began by studying a model of inquiring, reflective teaching, and then you practiced becoming an inquiring student of your own professional knowledge on three topics. You built on this constructivist learning by engaging in specific collaborative activities, and you used the model of reflective teaching as a service ideal for case study analysis. Finally, you examined power in everyday social relations in light of norms for teaching professionalism. You began by studying a model of teaching service and ended by studying professional leadership based on this model.

You have completed a highly responsible inquiry progression. Becoming a caring teacher means resisting the historical forces that bind teachers to semi-professionalism and professionism. This is the professional direction this text has taken by interpreting teaching as an exciting career challenge and a vital social service.

If such an historic undertaking seems to be too challenging at times, keep your focus on manageable day-to-day events—but don't lose sight of your goal. Imagine what it would be like if your generation of teachers could prepare the next generation of adults to function as active students of their best selves! Think of the impact you can have as an empowered professional in the classroom, in your school and local community, and in our society. Isn't this possibility worth the struggle as an inquiring educator?

Endnotes

1. For further study of the concept of professionalism, read Kultgen, J. (1988). *Ethics and Professionalism.* Philadelphia: University of Philadelphia Press.
2. For a critical analysis of bureaucratic assumptions from the point of view of teacher empowerment, see Beyer, L. E., & Apple, M. W. (Eds.). (1988). *The curriculum: problems, politics, and possibilities.* Albany, NY: State University of New York Press.
3. For an important case study of this type of socialization, see Willis, P. (1977). *Learning to labour: How working class kids get working class jobs.* Lexington, MA: D. C. Heath.

4. For an overview of the teacher empowerment movement in the United States, see Maeroff, G. (1988). *The empowerment of teachers: Overcoming the crisis of confidence.* New York: Macmillan.
5. Diercks, K., Dillard, S., McElliott, K., Morgan, J., Shulz, B., Tipps, L., & Wallentine, K. (1988). *Teacher leadership: Commitment and challenge* (p. 7). Seattle: Puget Sound Educational Consortium.
6. The Coalition of Essential Schools has member institutions in California, Connecticut, Florida, Iowa, Kentucky, Maine, Maryland, Massachusetts, Missouri, New Hampshire, New York, Pennsylvania, Rhode Island, South Carolina, Texas, Tennessee, Washington, Wisconsin, Vermont, and Alberta, Canada. For more information, contact the Coalition of Essential Schools, Brown University, Education Department, Box 1938, Providence, RI 02912.

References

APPLE, M. W. (1982). *Education and power.* Boston: Routledge and Kegan Paul.

BARTH, R. S. (1980). *Run school run.* Cambridge, MA: Harvard University Press.

BOWLES, S., & GINTIS, H. (1976). *Schooling in capitalistic America: Educational reform and the contradictions of economic life.* New York: Basic Books.

CALLAHAN, R. E. (1962). *Education and the cult of efficiency.* Chicago: University of Chicago Press.

DARLING-HAMMOND, L. (1988). Accountability and teacher professionalism. *American Educator, 12*(4), 8-13, 38–43.

DARLING-HAMMOND, L., & BERRY, B. (1988). *The evolution of teacher policy* (R3608-CPRE/CSTB). Santa Monica, CA: The Rand Corporation.

DEVANEY, K., & SYKES, G. (1988). Making the case for professionalism. In A. Lieberman (Ed.), *Building a professional culture in schools* (pp. 3–22). New York: Teachers College Press.

FOSTER, W. (1986). *Paradigms and promises: New approaches to educational administration.* Buffalo, NY: Prometheus Books.

GOODMAN, J. (1988). The political tactics and teaching strategies of reflective, active preservice teachers. *The Elementary School Journal, 89*(1), 23–40.

HOLMES GROUP, THE. (1990). *Tomorrow's schools.* East Lansing, MI: Author.

HOUSTON, H. M. (1988). Restructuring secondary schools. In A. Lieberman (Ed.), *Building a professional culture in schools* (pp. 109–128). New York: Teachers College Press.

JUDGE, H. (1988). Afterword. In A. Lieberman (Ed.), *Building a professional culture in schools* (pp. 222–231). New York: Teachers College Press.

LACEY, C. (1977). *The socialization of teachers.* London: Methuen.

LEVINE, M. (1988). Introduction. *Professional practice schools: Building a model* (pp. 1–25). Washington, D. C.: American Federation of Teachers' Center for Restructuring Educational Issues Department.

LIEBERMAN, A. (Ed.).(1988). *Building a professional culture in schools.* New York: Teachers College Press.

LORTIE, D. C. (1975). *Schoolteacher: A sociological study.* Chicago: University of Chicago Press.

MARSHALL, H. M. (1988). Work or learning: Implications of classroom metaphors. *Educational Researcher, 17*(9), 9–16.

Marshall, J. D., & SEARS, J. T. (1990). An evolutionary and metaphorical journey into teaching and thinking about curriculum. In J. T. Sears & J. D. Marshall (Eds.), *Teaching and thinking about curriculum: Critical inquiries* (pp. 15–38). New York: Teachers College Press.

MEIER, D. (1987). Success in East Harlem: How one group of teachers built a school that works. *American Educator, 11*(3), 34–39.

METZGER, W. P. (1987). A spectre haunts American scholars: The spectre of "professionism." *Educational Researcher, 16*(6), 10–18.

SERGIOVANNI, T. J. (1990). *Value-added leadership: How to get extraordinary performance in schools.* San Diego: Harcourt Brace Jovanovich.

SIZER, T. R. (1984). *Horace's compromise: The dilemma of the American high school.* Boston: Houghton Mifflin.

SOCKETT, H. (1983). Towards a professional code in teaching. In P. Gordon (Ed.), *Is teaching a profession?* (pp. 26–43). London: University of London Bedford Way Papers #15.

SYKES, G. (1987). Reckoning with the spectre. *Educational Researcher, 16*(6), 19–21.

Glossary

Academic Problem Solving: educational problem solving that is guided by a scholarly approach to instructional content; concern that students are properly introduced to the structure of an academic discipline.

Accommodative Resistance: the practice of publicly complying with school policy while privately seeking ways to function as an empowered professional.

Active Problem Solving: continuously alert approach to identifying and solving classroom learning problems.

Artistic Problem Solving: imaginatively adapting curriculum to meet students' background, interests, and needs.

Best Self: an ideal vision of what a person could become.

Bounded Problem: a problem that is relatively clear with a solution that is readily apparent to teachers with different beliefs and habits.

Classroom Community Leader: a teacher who consciously helps students develop democratic values while managing a class.

Classroom Norms: standards of behavior for a democratic classroom community.

Clustering: a brainstorming process to discover feelings and images about teaching.

Confirmation: understanding and supporting a person's best self.

Constructivist Approach to Learning: helping students actively construct meaning during learning by relating new knowledge to their past experiences and personal purposes.

Contemplative Practice: reflecting on personal, philosophical issues; raising questions about the wisdom of a course of action.

Contributive Inquiry: questioning that is guided by civic ethics; the goal is to be socially constructive.

Cooperative Learning: educational growth fostered by socially interactive activities.

Cooperative Practice: working cooperatively with students and parents.

Criterion-referenced Test: a test that explicitly relates what is being measured to what has been taught.

Critical Compliance: the practice of critically examining disruptions to teacher empowerment without immediately taking action to rectify the inequity.

Curriculum Leader: a teacher who becomes actively involved in deciding curriculum issues related to his or her classroom activities.

Curriculum Platform: a personal guide to curriculum development that considers content selection, content organization, and evaluation in terms of the teacher's own vision of what the curriculum should be.

Developmental Discipline: a classroom management approach in which students share responsibility for determining community norms and values and finding solutions for problems.

Dialogue: open, honest communication.

Discipline: learning to function as a responsible member of a democratic learning community. This type of learning is facilitated by the leadership of the teacher. This sense of social discipline can also be thought of as reciprocal, fair-minded self-discipline.

Educational Inquiry: a questioning, democratic perspective on the virtues of teaching and learning; a willingness to challenge any educational discourse.

Educational Problem Solving: imaginatively following the ethic of caring and the constructivist approach in solving students' learning problems.

Empirically Based Problem Solving: educational problem solving that is guided by a concern that students perform well on achievement tests.

Empowerment: a personal process of meaning making in which the individual acts openly and responsibly on his or her own interpretations of events.

Ethic of Caring: belief that teachers must care for and seek to understand their students as individuals and as learners with their own unique perspectives.

Expert Teacher: an active classroom problem solver who facilitates constructivist learning.

Expressive Writing: a technique to explore personal metaphors.

Historically Aware Problem Solving: educational problem solving that is guided by concern for the historical and social factors that encourage and inhibit equitable learning.

Instructional Objective: statement of expected learning outcome that defines terminal behavior, conditions under which behavior should occur, and acceptable performance level.

Intuitive Problem Solving: educational problem solving that is guided by concerns for student-teacher rapport; sensitivity to qualitative aspects of learning.

Learning Community: a group of individuals who respect one another's unique educational outlooks and who support and challenge one another to be lifelong learners.

Metacognition: the conscious monitoring of one's thought processes.

Metacognitive Strategy: the conscious use of a guide to thinking (or a thinking scaffold) to facilitate reflective or inquiring processes.

Normative Environment: an environment that provides models of appropriate values and actions.

Positive Freedom: the understanding that individual rights are exercised in the context of community responsibilities.

Power Over: the successful or unsuccessful attempt to control someone else's interpretation of events.

Professionalism: an orientation to complex work (such as teaching) that recognizes the values of active meaning-making, lifelong learning, and client service.

Professionism: a work ideology oriented towards status, power, and money.

Reflective Teaching: teaching characterized by practicing an ethic of caring, a constructivist approach to learning, and artistic problem solving. The reflective teacher considers the students' past experiences and personal purposes when introducing instructional content.

Self-actualization: the attainment of one's highest potential.

Semi-professionalism: work that takes place in a setting carefully controlled through top-down accountability policies.

Standard Knowledge Base: general prescriptions on good teaching that provide the "standard" for professional competence.

Task Analysis: process for breaking complex learning behaviors into component parts.

Technical Rationality: a rote, unimaginative approach to problem solving involving the use of standardized techniques to solve a problem.

Transformative Action: the practice of initiating major steps to openly function as an empowered teacher or professional; steps may be individual or collegial in nature.

Transformative Teaching: teaching with the ultimate goal of creating a better society.

Unbounded Problem: a complex problem that can legitimately be defined or tackled in many different ways.

Index

About the Contributors

JAMES G. HENDERSON is an Associate Professor at Kent State University, and he received his doctorate in Curriculum and Teaching from Stanford University. His publications have concentrated on teacher education and curriculum studies topics, and he has a leadership role in Kent State's diverse Professional Development School projects. His interests include reflective practice, curriculum theory, and teacher education reform. He is faculty advisor for Students for Professional Teaching, an undergraduate student organization at Kent State. Professor Henderson received a national award for the curriculum theory underlying this text.

CAROL R. MELNICK is an Assistant Professor and Chairperson of the Department of Special Education at National–Louis University. She began her professional career as a speech-language pathologist and received her doctorate in education from the University of Illinois at Chicago. Her publications have focused on topics relating to parent-teacher partnerships, the out-of-school curriculum, and teacher lore. Her professional interests include early childhood special education and the articulation of special and regular education.

THOMAS E. BARONE is an Associate Professor at Arizona State University, and he received his doctorate in Curriculum and Teaching from Stanford University. He has contributed to educational journals and books on a variety of contemporary curriculum topics. His primary interests are in the areas of curriculum theory, design, and evaluation.

MARI E. KOERNER is an Assistant Professor and Director of Teacher Education at Roosevelt University. She began her professional career as a

Chicago Public School teacher and received her doctorate in education from the University of Illinois at Chicago. Her publications have focused on topics related to teacher education, and she places a high priority on community service in the Chicago metropolitan area.

PATRICIA M. HERTEL is an Assistant Professor and Director for the Health Information Technology Program at Truman College, one of the Chicago City Colleges. She received her M.A. in Adult Education from Roosevelt University. She has numerous publications in the field of medical records and has contributed to literary journals and music and film periodicals. She is a practicing artist, and her paintings have been exhibited in art shows in Chicago.